IN PRAI‌

COVID-19/MENTAL

D1027644

"Ron Parks, MD has written a wonderful guidebook on how to navigate through life's traumas, emotional turmoils and crises. Using the upheaval of the pandemic, Dr. Parks offers clarity and insights for ways to change ourselves that minimize prescription drugs and instead offer core lifestyle, mindfulness, and spiritual solutions. He includes many heartfelt stories, including from his own life, showing us the power of using simple approaches to rebuild a better life. This very readable book gives you the tools and inspiration for achieving lasting changes, which can bring inner peace even in the midst of great disruption such as the pandemic."

—**Michael Rossoff, L.Ac**

"This book is a thoughtful, timely, and comprehensive resource for the many people who are impacted by the emerging mental health crises brought on by the COVID-19 pandemic. Dr. Parks offers a holistic framework for transforming adversity into an opportunity for growth, spanning significant topics such as neuroscience and spirituality. His approach to the problem brings hope without providing simplistic solutions. Members of the general public and healthcare practitioners can benefit from this book, which presents an overview of the important issues and a path toward individual and societal healing."

—**Larry Cammarata, Ph.D., Clinical Psychologist Director of Education, Mindfulness Travels**

"Dr. Parks has written a necessary and practical book on the coronavirus pandemic along with the concomitant consequences: fear, anxiety, trauma, and depression. Layered throughout the book are specific cases to support his contentions. He favors a holistic approach as a remedy as opposed to traditional medicine, emphasizing diet, exercise, and spirituality. This book is a must on your bookshelf considering these threatening and perilous times."

—**Arthur Laupus, Faculty-Osher Institute, Johns Hopkins University**

COVID-19
MENTAL HEALTH CRISES

Holistic Understanding and Solutions

Ronald R. Parks, MPH, MD

PARKSPRESS

Published by ParksPress.

Publisher's Cataloging-in-Publication data
Names: Parks, Ronald R., author.
Title: Covid-19 mental health crises : holistic understanding and solutions / Ronald R. Parks, MPH, MD.
Description: Includes bibliographical references. | Asheville, NC: ParksPress, 2021.
Identifiers: LCCN: 2021903815 | ISBN: 978-1-7365525-0-6 (paperback) | 978-1-7365525-1-3 (ebook)
Subjects: LCSH COVID-19 (Disease)--United States--21st century. | COVID-19 (Disease)--Social aspects--United States--21st century. | Epidemics--United States--21st Century. | Post-traumatic stress disorder--Treatment. | Psychic trauma--Treatment. | Post-traumatic stress disorder--Alternative treatment. | Psychic trauma--Alternative treatment. | BISAC HEALTH & FITNESS / Mental Health | HEALTH & FITNESS / Diseases (Contagious) | MEDICAL / Holistic Medicine | PSYCHOLOGY / Mental Health | HEALTH & FITNESS / Healing
Classification: LCC RA644.C67 .P37 2021 | DDC 362.1962/414--dc23

Editors: Laura E. Pasquale, Ph.D.; Shan E. Parks, BS

Cover design & interior formatting: Mark Thomas / Coverness.com

DISCLAIMER

This book's following writing and chapters are for informational and educational purposes only, not medical or mental health advice. The reader's responsibility is to direct personal medical or mental health questions to their primary care provider and specialty physicians. The information and statements contained in this material are not intended to diagnose, treat, cure, or prevent any disease or to replace the recommendations or advice given to you by your primary or direct care providers. Your reliance on any information provided by Dr. Parks is solely at your discretion. You are advised not to disregard medical advice from your primary or direct care providers or delay seeking medical advice or treatment because of the information contained in this book. Management of severe mental or physical health problems should remain under your primary care physicians, specialist, or psychiatrist's care and guidance.

TABLE OF CONTENTS

ACKNOWLEDGMENT
AND DEDICATION

This book is dedicated with gratitude to the devoted scientists who have been on the frontiers of discoveries and developments leading to new life-saving medications, rapid testing for control of viral spread, and vaccines. Also, appreciation goes to all the dedicated medical workers, doctors, healthcare workers, first responders, police, military, governors, mayors, public health, and civil servants who have bravely worked on behalf of the public good during this unprecedented health crisis. The greatest appreciation goes out to our fellow citizens and neighbors who have done their part in surviving one of the worst pandemics in recorded history.

A special remembrance goes to the many who have died or lost loved ones from illness related to COVID-19. This includes a dedication to Dan, a friend who lost a valiant fight with COVID-19, and to his wife Gloria, also infected, but a survivor of the illness, as she faces the loss of her beloved, lifelong partner.

Finally, a special thanks go out to the people instrumental in bringing my writing into a book form. These talented and very patient individuals include my son Shan Parks, a gifted writer; and my wife Jan, for her patience and thoughtful listening to my ideas and article drafts; my friends; colleagues; and the other professionals who helped with this project.

PREFACE

COVID-19, a novel virus (also referred to as SARS-CoV-2), has caused a global pandemic, death, and destruction in the U.S. and other countries. Life and our existing social behavior and lifestyle have most likely changed forever. As we have seen, the very contagious, new viral agent with many unknown characteristics can be deadly and incredibly infectious, especially among groups at high risk.

The significant amount of illness and the impact on peoples' lives has contributed to a failing economy. At the time of this writing, as the pandemic continues globally with a record number of new COVID-19 cases and deaths in the U.S., fear, anger, and bewilderment persist.

Simultaneously, with increases in the incidence of mental illness, the demands on community resources, and the ensuing mental health crises are similar to the impacts of natural disasters, losses, war, or other catastrophic events.

In this book, the coronavirus pandemic and other historical occurrences of losses, crises, disasters, and mental illnesses are discussed from holistic medicine and integrative psychiatry perspectives. Hopefully the presentation will provide practical information and wisdom to address mental health challenges during crises and tragedies.

Relief appears to be on the way with the Emergency Use Authorization (EUA) of three safe and effective SARS-CoV-2 vaccines, bringing the promise of controlling the virus and ending the pandemic.

Until then, let's stay well, stay safe, listen to accurate, credible information, make informed decisions, take the right actions, and be level-headed and calm amid any challenges now or in the future.

With appreciation for your interest,

Ron Parks, MPH MD
April 2021

PART I: HOLISTIC COPING

PANDEMIC, FEAR, AND ANXIETY

Dr. Sid* (endearingly called just "Sid" by the healthcare workers at the larger inner-city hospital where he had worked for the past fifteen years) carefully made his way through the nearly deserted city in the early morning darkness. It was an eerie scene of desolation and emptiness. He felt anxious and depressed, dreading what would soon face him, as he parked his car near the imposing four-story hospital structure.

Passing through the emergency room to get to his office on the second floor, he immediately noticed the anguish and terror in the faces of the many people sitting in chairs or on stretchers in long lines reaching out into the streets. The COVID-19 pandemic had caught everyone unprepared.

Walking towards the elevator, he had an increased, pounding heartbeat and an arising of suffocation, danger, and darkness, bringing with it a sense of doom and helplessness. Hidden deep in his memory, grotesque images emerged; these were scenes of his battlefield experiences, including witnessing people dying after a bomb had exploded in their compound. Nauseating flashbacks appeared of body parts strewed everywhere. As a medic, he had been overwhelmed, as there wasn't adequate medical personnel for the wounded and dying. He also remembered the sickening smell of burning flesh. Their small field hospital had failed to be

3

adequately prepared or equipped for that level of disaster. His final memory was of his attempting to find and triage the living and to salvage life, of blacking out, then waking up later in the field hospital with a minor head wound from flying shrapnel.

Refocusing, Sid adjusted his facemask and got onto the elevator, which was empty this time of the morning. He realized that he was nearing a breaking point, a product of all the stress of working in the overwhelming situation of caring for dying patients and witnessing so much death. The hospital and city were now in the worst part of the pandemic onset. Like many, his hospital had suffered from staffing losses and inadequate supplies and equipment to manage such an unexpected catastrophe. Also, he realized that his age now placed him in one of those high-risk groups for severe disease and death from the virus. He had experienced the reality of coping with life after loss with the death of his wife and son, and later his mother's dying from COVID-19. He realized now that he hadn't taken the time he needed or reached out for necessary help and support. Instead, his days had become mostly focused on his work, where he felt appreciated. And Sid had also become less active in his free time and had gained weight, exhibiting early signs of heart disease, high blood pressure, and diabetes.

After grabbing a cup of coffee and getting dressed in protective clothing and mask, Sid reached the intensive care unit for rounds with the nurse and new, young intern. They discussed the recent deaths of patients who had expired during the night. The three completed rounds about mid-morning, making some medication changes, examining patients, and writing new orders. Frantic families called to find out their loved ones' status, calls to which he would have to attend. On his way out of the ICU, Sid grabbed the list with the families' phone numbers so he could make calls either with the good news of progress, no change, or to report of downward turns or the death of loved ones.

Halfway down the hall to his office, Sid felt suddenly like an elephant was sitting on his chest—crushing the life and breath out of him—and he crumpled to the floor. The pain continued through his left arm and chest, and he had difficulty catching his breath. The next thing he knew, he was waking up in the coronary care unit. One of his younger colleagues, a cardiologist, told Sid that he was stable but had suffered a significant heart attack. Relieved, on the one hand, that he wasn't dying of COVID, he was also shocked by the major heart attack.

Lying in his hospital bed, Sid believed that his heart attack resulted from the overwhelming combination of culprits including stress, anxiety, aging, an undesirable lifestyle and remnants of his PTSD from war trauma, as well as residual grieving from the death of loved ones. Living and practicing in a pandemic, among so much devastation, had also triggered memories of many personal losses and reminders of his previous war experiences and of losing his home, wife, and young son during a hurricane.

Fortunately, Sid survived his heart attack and even experienced a bit of an awakening about changing his lifestyle. Now he could find a more suitable and less demanding work situation. Sid had also appreciated the young intern who came to visit and spent time with him on the coronary care unit. Both could listen to each other and share their individual life stories, with their respective trials and tribulations, the good and bad times, losses and blessings, and what could still be valued in gratitude.

As they shared, the young intern cried; his wife had recently suffered the stillbirth of what was to have been their first child. And so Sid realized that it was a blessing for both of them to share and talk. The presence of the young intern also reminded him of the son he had lost. After he left the hospital, Sid kept track of the young doctor, later becoming an appreciated support and mentor for the intern and was treated as a family member.

(*To protect confidentiality, stories in this book are composites of clinical experiences and do not represent actual persons.)

THE IMPACT OF THE CORONAVIRUS (COVID-19)

The rapid spread and potential for severe illness brought by COVID-19 have dramatically increased anxiety, depression, associated diseases, and deaths. While some fear and anxiety probably help motivate people to adhere to public health guidelines (to prevent getting the virus, carrying the virus, and infecting other people), too much stress can also lower immunity, reduce the amount of needed restorative sleep, and increase infection vulnerability. Such emotional distress and mental impairment can also cause a loss of work time, disruptions in relationships, drug addictions, overdoses, and suicides. The less anxious or (perhaps worse) the misinformed people who ignore basic public health guidelines can contribute to the loss of control of the viral spread, with all its dire consequences.

Besides impairing immunity, anxiety can lead to increased hoarding or over isolation. People might get needed supplies in order to stay at home and to avoid risky public venues. However, in these anxious times, the risk is to become obsessed and addicted to watching too much TV, consuming news reports that feed fear and worry while offering limited practical information about disease prevention or control.

For those feeling overwhelmed in the current crisis, with symptoms of increasing anxiety, panic, or obsessiveness, this may be the time to consider getting support or outside help. Cascading emotional distress might otherwise contribute to emotional collapse and severe depression; therefore, **recognizing and managing fear and anxiety is essential to maintaining healthy emotions and moods.**

MANY PEOPLE DON'T SEEK OR RECEIVE HELP

Anxiety disorders affect 40 million adults, or 18.1% of the U.S. population, every year during typical, non-coronavirus times, making anxiety the most common mental/emotional/psychological condition in our country. Anxiety and related disorders account for a significant portion of the U.S.

mental health budget. A considerable number of people with an anxiety disorder also have at least one other accompanying psychiatric condition. These disorders can cause overwhelming, debilitating anxiety and fear that can become worse if not treated. And yet *less than 30% of individuals with these problems seek treatment, and many go undiagnosed by their primary healthcare providers.*[1]

FEAR

Fear can paralyze a person through a loss of productivity, of effectiveness, and of quality of life. And today's unique atmosphere of a viral COVID-19 pandemic is overwhelming for many. Even with stimulus packages enacted, our nation is experiencing a collapsing economy. In the face of these events, unchecked fear and worry can build to a loss of confidence, insecurity, and significant emotional states, including anxiety, panic, and depression.

Mental Health America (MHA) has been conducting online screenings for six years, and with over 5.5 million completed, it's the United States' most extensive screening program. Data from their recent online mental health screen showed a significantly greater moderate-to-severe depression or anxiety rate than in a similar study before the pandemic. A quarter of study participants cited grief, loss, and financial concerns as contributors to anxiety and depression. Current events appeared as a significant factor in the development of mental health problems as well. Respondents who screened positive for depression reported increased thoughts of suicide or self-harm on at least half of the days and up to nearly every day.

According to a two-month July 2020 survey from the reputable Kaiser Family Foundation, more than half of the U.S. population have experienced adverse effects from COVID-19-related stress. The question asked was, "Has worry or stress caused you to experience any of the following in the past two months?" followed by a list of health effects. Frequently reported difficulties included problems with sleep, poor appetite or overeating, mental health issues, headaches, stomachaches, temper difficulties, increased alcohol, drug use, and worsening of existing chronic illnesses such as diabetes and hypertension.

PEOPLE WORRY ABOUT SUSTAINING THEMSELVES AND THEIR FAMILIES

Since the onset of the pandemic, the weakened economy has wiped out the five prior years of economic growth, driving fears of a more prolonged recovery, as was seen during the Great Depression. With growing unemployment, losses of businesses and jobs, and uncertain access to government-funded aid, the current surge in coronavirus cases and deaths in the U.S. and concern about further business shutdowns have led to decreases in consumer confidence and spending.

ANXIETY AND FEAR CAN SOAR

Faced with the many new demands and measures needed for surviving the pandemic, anxiety and fear can soar for many people. These demands include:

- Avoiding close personal contact with social distancing
- Wearing masks
- Doing frequent hand washing and sanitizing of surfaces
- Staying out of closed spaces occupied by potential coronavirus carriers, such as places of usual recreation, eating or drinking, shopping, working, and entertainment

WHO IS SUSCEPTIBLE?

People who are more apt to have heightened worries are older individuals, people with medical issues like smoking, chronic airway disease, obesity, diabetes, and individuals living in high-risk environments such as nursing homes or crowded spaces. Essential workers and people who have gone back to work are always aware (or at least they should be!) of the safety measures needed to prevent spreading the virus. Therefore, stress and fears can be an overwhelming reality; these are already frequently higher in disadvantaged, minority communities and amongst essential workers where higher rates of COVID illnesses and deaths occur.

Contributors to a higher spread of the COVID-19 virus are poverty, lack of healthcare resources, living in less healthy environments, and the existence of health vulnerabilities such as obesity, diabetes, and hypertension. Also, the economic disparity of people in the U.S. living below the poverty line will most likely increase as the current pandemic continues and unemployment grows. With the supply of basics such as food and shelter threatened, fear, anxiety, and panic will probably increase among the disadvantaged. Higher demands will then occur on the government and on all able citizens to create an increased flow of opportunities and financial help for such individuals and communities in need. Thus, getting past the current crisis will require the best leadership and personal efforts to address these critical issues and threats to well-being.

Individuals are also more prone to anxiety and mood disturbances if they have a prior history of significant trauma. The residual effects of traumatization occur in individuals who have experienced life-threatening situations, losses, or severe illness, or who are victims of or witnesses of violence, near-death experiences, auto accidents, exposure to natural disasters or war, earlier life deprivations, or abuse. Post-traumatic stress disorder (PTSD) is an example of the recurrence of anxiety states and related physical and emotional symptoms from such residual prior traumatic experiences.

THE BEST STRATEGIES

Like the risk of getting a COVID-19 infection when in a closed space with other infected people, fear and anxiety can likewise rise dramatically by being "caged-in" or stuck in one's inner thoughts and emotions. Levels of fear and anxiety can also become compounded when individuals are caught in tight quarters with others who are experiencing fearful states. Avoiding getting help, counseling, or therapy, especially if there is a history of unresolved trauma from the past, will increase the likelihood of developing severe mental health issues or illness.

Those having a history of trauma or living with others who have an unchecked emotional or mental illness should seek help or guidance early, preferably as soon as they experience growing fear, worry, or anxiety. Early identification of feelings or symptoms of unhealthy emotional or mood states is an initial step in knowing when to get help or support. Prompt attention and early intervention may also prevent the progression of persisting fear and worry toward more severe and chronic disruptions in one's well-being and mental health, such as continuing anxiety and depression conditions.

BE ALERT TO THE SIGNS

Signs of anxiety may include:

- Being frequently nervous, irritable, moody, or on edge
- Feeling a sense of impending danger or doom
- Increased or rapid pulse/heart rate, palpitations, and dizziness
- Fast or troubled breathing and sweating
- Increase tiredness, weakness, and wanting to sleep more
- Muscle tension, fatigue, and trembling
- Difficulty concentrating and getting things done
- Having trouble sleeping, with more frequent nightmares
- Experiencing digestive problems and changes in appetite
- Panic attacks, which appear suddenly and increase in intensity over several minutes, peak, and usually go rapidly away

If any of these symptoms persist, please consider seeking appropriate support.

PANIC ATTACKS

Panic attacks can occur due to growing anxiety. Panic differs from fear and other types of anxiety. They include severe anxiety, muscle tightness, trembling, fast heartbeat, fast or troubled breathing, dizziness, impaired concentration, palpitations, sweating, and sleep disturbances. Also, panic attacks are often unprovoked, appearing suddenly and increasing in intensity over several minutes, peaking, and then rapidly subsiding over 20 to 30 minutes. An episode can occur as a one-time event or can repeatedly occur, triggered by something remembered, or it can appear without warning, and occasionally when awakening from sleep. These episodes can be very disruptive, disturbing, and disabling. One explanation for the cause of the panic attacks is that the body's typical alarm system of mental and physical responses to an actual threat, the "fight-or-flight response," gets triggered and activated even when there is no real threat present.

MOUNTING ANXIETY AND FEAR

In "normal" times, panic attacks possibly occur in 20% of the U.S. population at least once in their lifetimes, or in 3% of the population at any given time. With the heightened fears over illness and related concerns (personal and family safety, work, career, paying the bills, getting needed food, shelter, medications, etc.), panic attacks are likely to become more prevalent and widespread. By altering support systems, the usual public health measures to prevent the spread of illness (such as social distancing, sheltering in place, and avoidance of community activities) could make some more vulnerable to panic episodes.

Identified causal or contributing factors to panic attacks include:

- An actual or transient medical problem such as a middle ear infection, allergies, mitral valve prolapse (often a mild dysfunction of this heart valve closure), hyperthyroidism, or low blood sugar
- Earlier life history of significant trauma or post-traumatic stress

disorder, with embedded memories of prior trauma, increase
susceptibility for panic episodes in an already highly anxious and
hypervigilant person

- Medications use or withdrawal, stimulant or substance use, or abuse
  (caffeine, alcohol, opiates, etc.) can lead to greater vulnerability to
  panic attacks

- Overuse of stimulants like caffeine or non-prescribed or unnecessary
  stimulant drugs, or drugs of abuse as methamphetamine or cocaine

- Life events involving significant stress, losses, threats of damage, or
  the feelings of increased vulnerability may precede panic attacks, such
  as the current mounting fears over the coronavirus

Panic disorder can become recurrent and disabling. If the panic episode
occurs in a specific setting, as in a store or car, irrational fears or phobias about
these situations may arise. If a person avoids these situations, he or she can
become increasingly housebound, unable to drive, and develop agoraphobia
(fear of public places). If the person doesn't receive effective early treatment,
increasing incapacitation in life activities can result.

PAST TRAUMA

The American Psychological Association (APA) defines trauma as "an
emotional response to a terrible event like an accident, rape or natural disaster."
They continue: "Immediately after the event, shock and denial are typical.
Longer-term reactions include unpredictable emotions, flashbacks, strained
relationships and even physical symptoms like headaches or nausea. While
these feelings are normal, some people have difficulty moving on with their
lives."[2]

Significant trauma also is a situation or event that may be recurrent, as
can happen with severe emotional or physical abuse. The original, horrifying
experience is usually coupled with the overwhelming fear that one's life, physical
safety, or psychological integrity is at risk, without the ability to defend one's

self or to survive intact. The full emotional or physical reaction to the event or situation happens either immediately or later on.

COPING WITH DEPRESSION

Depression has similarly increased during the COVID-19 pandemic, either with or without anxiety and panic attacks. Signs of significant depression may include:

- Feeling down, guilt, hopeless, helpless, sad, or irritable ("pushing people away" or not getting along with others)
- Loss of one's usual interests or pleasure in doing things (anhedonia)
- Changes in sleep patterns, such as trouble falling asleep, not getting restful sleep, sleeping too much, not wanting to get up, or staying in bed much of the day
- Feeling tired, a loss of vitality, or having little energy
- Poor appetite, overeating, weight loss or gain
- Frequently feeling bad about oneself, such as feeling worthless or as a failure
- Trouble concentrating or remembering things
- Slowing down of speech or movements and/or having a frequent sad face
- Being fidgety or restless more than usual
- Difficulty functioning at home or work
- Withdrawal and isolating self from others
- Spending more time on TV, computers, tablets, or cell phones
- Being preoccupied with watching movies or the news
- Thoughts of dying, self-harm (suicidal thoughts), or harming others (homicidal thoughts)

All the listed symptoms or behaviors of anxiety, depression, or panic attacks may be only slightly present, noticed at times, or be very pervasive in a severely affected person's daily life and activity. If a person feels that life has lost its meaning and is not worth living and/or has suicidal thoughts or feelings about hurting oneself or others, it is time to act and seek outside help from a qualified mental healthcare professional or resource.

For immediate or crisis help, call your local suicide hotline (1-800-273-8255, 1-800-273-TALK, 1-800-273-8255), or 1-800-SUICIDE (1-800-784-2433) for the National Suicide Prevention Lifeline.

REMEMBER THE CHILDREN!

Children are also susceptible to COVID-19 infections. There is a growing recognition that the younger part of the population is also at significant risk for fear, anxiety, and mood problems during these pandemic times. Signs and symptoms of impending trouble might be different for children than that seen in adults. Such behavior or emotional changes in children might include:

- Temper tantrums, acting-out behaviors as being destructive, getting into fights or arguments
- Sleep difficulties and nightmares
- Showing decreased interests in things they usually enjoyed
- Being more sullen or apathetic or becoming more hyperactive
- Not wanting to take part in playful or recreational activities with themselves or with others
- Not eating well, gaining or losing weight
- Loss of concentration, attention, and becoming more distractible

Some of these children's changes may be a warning sign for seeking support or help for the younger at-risk and vulnerable family members. **Early recognition, getting support, and seeking assistance is critical for preventing and reducing the risk of chronic emotional and mental impairments and related physical illnesses.**[3]

HOLISTIC, HUMANISTIC, TRANSPERSONAL, OR HOLOTROPIC THERAPIES

When severe and recurrent fear and anxiety persist, help and relief can be possible with an effective therapeutic intervention. Ideally, the intervention helps the person to:

- Get unstuck from unhealthy patterns of behavior, rigid beliefs, and fearful or painful memories.
- Reduce or eliminate anxiety, panic, addictions, and trauma-related symptoms.
- Focus more on the present and the here and now, rather than the past or future.
- Become more present, mindful, and aware.
- Improve energy, focus, concentration, daily functioning, and skills to prevent relapse or recurring symptoms.
- Develop greater acceptance and compassion.
- Regain the wisdom and the balance of personal power, self-needs, and the needs of others.
- Reestablish social support and networks.

Therapies are often benefcical for anxiety, mood impairments, and prior trauma, such as Eye Movement Desensitization and Reprocessing (EMDR) and Cognitive-Behavioral Therapy (CBT) interventions.[4] Holistic, humanistic, transpersonal, or holotropic therapies may involve:

- Education about the body's physiological reaction to fear and threat
- Use of experiential techniques, talk/listening, person to person, and group therapies
- Desensitization to the various physical sensations or triggers of panic through the exposure of a person to the actual object, situation, or thought
- Catastrophic-thought-reducing techniques
- Learning relaxation, breathing, and stress management techniques
- Restructuring dysfunctional thoughts and patterns

- Gaining personal insights and the realization of one's inner strength and vision to overcome obstacles
- Transforming from being the victim of a horrible traumatic experience and memories to a broader perception of life, one's power, and potentialities
- Acceptance that the mind is continually moving toward the healing of its own emotional and mental health
- A personal commitment to supporting the healing process and therapeutic work as needed
- Supporting the person's process and strengths to release frozen past traumatic memories and constricting defenses, to regain energy flow and vitality
- Help for regaining flexibility and getting unstuck from rigid core beliefs and attitudes, in order to experience an expanded vision and perspective about life outside of the narrow constraints of a limiting mind-ego

Such approaches can help an individual to reduce stress and anxiety.

UNDERLYING MEDICAL CONDITIONS

Unfortunately, healthcare providers are often not familiar with the potentially devastating and disabling effect of the improper treatment of anxiety-related conditions. Management of anxiety is usually done with a tranquilizer, an antidepressant, or reassurance by a conventional healthcare practitioner. A thorough evaluation by a qualified medical and mental health practitioner with skills and expertise in working with anxiety, panic, and mood difficulties is often warranted, helpful, and is a better route when available. Finding caring and valuable help, when possible, may get at the deeper issues and the roots of anxiety conditions, rather than simply suppressing symptoms.

Holistic and natural therapies can be the most effective treatment course when combined with more traditional treatment. Some positive complementary approaches for consideration are:

- Lifestyle modifications and life skill enhancements
- Mind, body, and spiritual practice such as yoga; chi gong; mindfulnes; meditation; creative arts; or exercise with mindfulness as running, swimming, biking, or dance
- Stress management and relaxation techniques
- Acupuncture and massage therapies
- Targeted nutritional therapies, botanical medicine, nutritional education about dietary choices, and micronutrients (as with herbs, vitamins, minerals, essential fatty acids, and even amino acids—the smallest units of protein and a precursor of brain neurotransmitters, which can sometimes help relieve anxiety and milder depression in combination with other natural and complementary therapies)

Medication may also be of value in resistant or severe emotional or mental health conditions, such as major depression, if natural treatments have not worked. Antidepressants or tranquilizers used by conventional medical practitioners can sometimes bring more immediate relief. However, their long-term use is controversial due to the possibility to cause other medical issues. Once in use, trying to stop medication can lead to relapse or, with some tranquilizing drugs or alcohol, can cause withdrawal seizures. Thus, medicines may not have the same lasting effect and benefits as useful therapy programs and natural alternatives.

TIPS: TWENTY-ONE INTENTIONAL WAYS TO REDUCE ANXIETY

1. Reduce the time watching shows, checking social media, or listening to news stories on your TV, computer, or smartphone when home or in the workplace. Check only once or twice per day to keep informed. Pick unbiased and truthful news outlets that do not have partisan political ties. Avoid misinformation or politically motivated reporting

about the virus, pandemics, or politics. Hearing about the problems repeatedly during the day can lead to increased worry, anxiety, tension, poor sleep, or worse.

2. Instead of too much inactivity, such as passive watching, listening, or obsessing about current worries or events, take frequent time-outs with regular exercise. Active movement includes stretching and eating healthy meals (avoiding sweet binging and over-snacking on high-sugar and high-caloric food or drinks). Enjoy periodic relaxation times with deep breathing, meditation, or yoga. Sleep to get adequate restorative rest.

3. Cut down or stop smoking or vaping, which put you at higher risk for a COVID-19 infection. Use a nicotine patch if necessary.

4. Avoid alcohol and non-prescription drugs.

5. If working from home or in the workplace, take more frequent breaks, stand more, or take outside walks.

6. Keep to a regular exercise schedule such as 15 to 30 minutes one to two times per day. Beneficial exercise can take many forms. Examples are walking, biking, walking stairs, housework, or an exercise routine. Other choices are taking part in an online group exercise program, or in a circuit exercise routine, including push-ups, lunges, jumping jacks, and running in place. Do relax, enjoy, and allow any worries and fears to move to the background of your awareness as you fully embrace the physical movement, breathing, and letting go of tension.

7. After doing an excellent exercise routine, you can treat yourself to a nice hot bath with two or three cups of Epsom salt and a few drops of essential oils as lavender oil to melt away any remaining tension.

8. Get outside and into natural settings. Being in and closer to nature is very calming and healing. Move, breathe, take in the beauty and harmony that abounds around us.

9. Get involved with enjoyable recreational or artistic activities like art,

writing, and craftwork. It is the time for creative homeschooling if you have children.

10. Read an excellent book.

11. Complete home construction projects or prepare new recipes and meals.

12. Enjoy listening to music, dancing, or watching a good movie.

13. Complete a crossword or jigsaw puzzle.

14. Watch a comedy show for some humor and laughs.

15. Stay socially connected with friends, family, and community through video chats, texts, emails, phone calls, or social-distanced meetings, with face masks, if needed. Share your concerns about what you're experiencing. Value what has made you laugh amidst all the outside turmoil.

16. Learn or do yoga, mindfulness practices, meditation, or beneficial exercise routines to help with stress reduction and relaxation. Look for some interesting instructional videos that you can watch online with your computer or smartphone.

17. If the time and resources are available, take part in an online virtual certification, continuing education, or a university degree program.

18. Let the current pandemic crisis—a time of significant disruption and travails—be a time to do an in-depth review of what is essential and meaningful. Meditate and reflect on what is beyond your fears and self-preoccupations. Be aware of our small but significant connection with everything outside of ourselves. Find some inspirational readings or online materials and teachings from the spiritual, mystical, or faith traditions.

19. Find some meaning and purpose in the turmoil and tragedy that surround us. Being more centered and grounded will bring better preparedness for what may unfold in the coming days, which may call for the strength and the spirit to do the best for yourself and others

while not giving in to fear or over-focusing on personal issues and losses. Allow the current crisis and stresses to inspire you towards living a simpler, more meaningful life, to serve better the greater good, the community, and the environment. Be encouraged to be socially active to bring about positive change.

20. Do absolutely nothing, be in the moment, breathe, take it all in that is, including trouble and worry, but also what is comforting, beautiful, and inspiring for you—all of that for which you can be thankful. Taking a respite, a time-out to refill your reserves, will help you to regain your resilience and strength, so that you can move on with purpose, gratitude, and hope.

21. Finding the best path for yourself to move through fear and anxiety is of central importance during these stressful times. Be constantly aware and get the help you need at the first signs of distress. Be prepared to offer service and support to others with emotional difficulties. This is the time for exceptional acceptance and compassion towards oneself and others as ever-changing feelings, emotionality, insecurities, and vulnerabilities challenge us.[5]

DEPRESSION AND GRIEF

"I am profoundly depressed. My wife of 50 years, Helen*, after a valiant fight, died in the ICU of a COVID-19 infection. The two of us were inseparable companions and had lived through many difficult times and challenges. Then, out of the blue, my dear wife developed a cough, shortness of breath, and difficulty breathing. Things progressed rapidly, and we ended up in the emergency room. The last time I saw my dear partner was on her way to the ICU for placement on a respirator. She bravely smiled at me with her parting glance. Helen died ten days later, and now there is only grief. The golden years to enjoy the fruits of our labors were no more. Now I can't get out of bed, don't feel like eating, and cry most of the time. Other family members and friends have tried to console me, but their attempts to help seem to make things worse. I feel like dying myself and joining my wife and even have had thoughts of taking all the pills in the bathroom cabinet. What can I do?"

(*Helen and her husband are not specific individuals but a composite of people with similar stories encountered in past clinical situations. My condolences and prayers go to the families and any others with painful losses during the pandemic.)

SYMPTOMS OF DEPRESSION AND GRIEF

The experiences of this widower went beyond the natural grieving process and rapidly progressed to a life-threatening condition, with the presence of suicidal thoughts with a plan. The appearance of deepening depression called for immediate steps. Because of the increasing symptoms of major depression (or in this situation, a significant pathological grieving process) associated with physical deterioration from not eating or sleeping, including weight loss, the person needed an immediate psychiatric and mental health evaluation. The evaluating psychiatrist felt that there might be a need for placement in a supervised setting with medical support, intensive therapy work (especially around the devastating loss of his spouse), and use of antidepressant medication as needed.

HEIGHTENED DEMAND FOR MENTAL HEALTH SERVICES

With a catastrophic pandemic and exposure to overwhelming circumstances, and a high number of deaths, survivors are at increased risk for anxiety, grief, major depression, and even post-traumatic stress disorder (PTSD). Simultaneously, mental health services are overwhelmed.

Heightened awareness of the signs and symptoms of significant depression or insurmountable grief is essential to reduce the illness and impacts to individuals and families. Recognition, help, and resources must be directed to those in need to prevent the adverse consequences of untreated post-trauma, major depression, and anxiety, including the heightened vulnerability to severe illnesses and death. Those affected by the COVID-19 pandemic also include the front-line medical workers, first responders, police, and those affected by the loss of a significant other.

With the current overwhelming number of deaths from the COVID-19 pandemic, mental health services and workers will be essential responders to help with the recovery of the many affected by loss and trauma. Like the regular medical community's ill-preparedness, mental health programs, resources, and trained providers are underfunded, and so are now inadequately prepared for such a high-demand crisis situation.[6] As a result, becoming more aware of mental health is crucial during such times.

In a sense, everyone now will become front-line workers because of the overwhelming need for people in the community and significant others to recognize severe life-threatening depression symptoms. The first step is to learn the early signs of depression, just as people learn how to recognize the onset of infections. Along with the recognition of depression, education is needed about preparedness, support measures, and emergency responses for a severe, life-threatening depressive condition.

STAGES OF GRIEF AND LOSS

Being supportive of someone with depression means understanding grief and loss stages better, as Kübler-Ross first presented.[7]

Elizabeth Kübler-Ross's book *On Death and Dying* introduced the five stages of grief and loss. Some aspects of these stages happen after losing a loved one or significant other.

1. **Denial:** Experiencing the denial stage happens after a loss, accompanied by intense feelings such as shock, disbelief, confusion, fear, avoidance, and emotional numbing. An avoidance occurs, by which an individual suppresses or represses painful thoughts or feelings into the unconscious. Sometimes, denial can be present to the extent that one goes on with everyday activities as if nothing significant happened. Other emotions or behaviors, sometimes associated with denial or different stages, are agitation (being "hyper" and highly anxious, or even happy) or an inflated sense of relief at being a survivor when others have died.

- **Anger:** An anger stage can occur, which begins as the reality of the loss returns. Emotions arise such as feelings of blame towards oneself or others, irritation, frustration, or nervousness. Anger arises about the unfairness of life: "Why did this have to happen to me?"

- **Bargaining**: During this stage, when guilt arises, being present, reflective, accepting, and open to the experience of the anger or other painful emotions is a healthy acknowledgment that it is a part of the grieving process. A person might bargain, "If I do more of this or that, work more, or pray more, or something, this pain and grief will go away, and I can go back to living my life." It is the time to reach out to others, to tell about or to reflect on the loss, painful happening, and remembrances, with the struggle to find meaning in "all of it."

- **Depression:** A depression stage can challenge individual endurance, especially when it shows up frequently or for prolonged periods.

- **Acceptance:** The acceptance stage occurs when the residual feeling of loss, sadness, and grief with the reality of death's finality comes into a balance with recognizing that life continues. This stage comes when one explores life choices and options without the valued companion or loved one. There is an acceptance that returning memories and feelings will appear when triggered by reminders, with varying intensity and time spans (months, years, and sometimes a lifetime). Many things can trigger a memory of the deceased such as a picture, a personal possession, a grooming aid, or at a time of doing a routine with the lost loved one. Sometimes a dream will trigger some aspect of the grieving process. Any reminder can be an opportunity for further reflection and for working through loss, grief, and painful emotions.

RECOVERY FROM PHYSICAL ILLNESS

Depression often exists with other conditions. This means that recovery from illness can be made more difficult unless depression recognition and treatment occur. As we've seen, major depression is one of the most disabling mental disorders in the U.S., and chronic diseases such as diabetes, pain, substance abuse, arthritis, hypertension, and heart disease worsen with depression.

Identification and treatment of depression may bring:

- Marked benefit in the form of medical improvement
- Enhanced quality of life
- Reduction in disability
- Progress in recovery and treatment compliance

DEPRESSION IS COSTLY

Healthcare costs for depression in the U.S., as well as the value of lost work, are enormous. Conversely, effective interventions for depression, including coexisting substance abuse or medical problems, lowers health care costs.

Depression can predate a medical or addiction problem, or it can occur as a reactive response to illness-related stress. Depression can also be related to the physiology of the illness, to treatment interventions, or to prescribed medications. In neurological conditions such as Parkinson's disease, multiple sclerosis, Alzheimer's disease, and strokes, the lifetime prevalence of depression is 30 to 60 percent, compared to a *much* lower percentage in the general population.

Similarly, in diabetes, the lifetime prevalence of depression is double or triple that of the general population. It can cause an increased insulin requirement and can increase the risk of diabetic complications. In addition, people with coronary artery disease and depression have a 40 percent higher risk of having a cardiac event. Depression increases the risk of death from a heart attack five-fold and is a significant predictor of disability one month after a heart attack or one year after coronary bypass surgery. Finally, substance abuse is linked to depression. Estimates of depression and cocaine dependence range from 33 to 53 percent. Estimates of depression in alcoholics seeking treatment range from 15 to 67 percent. Those who depend on opiates have rates of depression estimated as high as 75 percent.

Early diagnosis and treatment of depression are critical in preventing and easing sickness, suffering, and death. Some studies suggest that 30 to 50

percent of depressed patients go unrecognized in primary care settings—
and only about 20 percent of those recognized receive adequate treatment.
Health care providers, friends, family, and employers all need to make a more
significant effort. Community education about key signs of depression is
essential.

TIPS: RECOGNIZING SEVERE GRIEF AND DEPRESSION

Revisit this chapter on "Depression and Grief" for the symptoms and
behaviors of severe prolonged grief or depression. All the listed symptoms or
behaviors may be only slightly present, only sometimes noticeable, or very
pervasive in a depressed or grieving person's daily life and activity. Prolonged
severe grief is an indicator of major depression and the need for evaluation
and treatment.

When severe depression or grief is present, one can quickly drop back
into earlier stages of grief, such as denial, hostility, anger, avoidance, and
wishing to flee or run away from emotional discomfort. Perhaps a person
feels that life has lost its meaning and is not worth living and has suicidal
thoughts or feelings about hurting oneself or others. In that case, it is time to
act and to seek outside help from a qualified mental healthcare professional
or resource.[8]

**In the U.S., for immediate or crisis help, call your local suicide hotline
or 1-800-273-8255 1-800-273-TALK, for the National Suicide Prevention
Lifeline.**

PREDISPOSING FACTORS FOR MOOD DISTURBANCES

Identifying and treating contributing factors can be as crucial as getting help
from a therapist, taking medication, or other beneficial treatments. In addition
to grief, other conditions can predispose a person to grief. Consultation to
uncover risk factors or predisposition to significant emotional or depressive
illness is a place to start, preferably by working with a qualified mental health

or medical healthcare provider. Some predisposing or vulnerability factors could include:

- Medical issues such as difficulties with nutritional deficiencies, hormone deficiencies, hypothyroidism, diabetes, heart disease, or obesity

- Family (genetic history) of depression, or bipolar illness, or other mood conditions

- Adverse lifestyle such as inadequate nutrition, sedentary habits, and chaotic, stressful living, or working in adverse conditions

- Traumatic brain injury, chronic pain, multiple surgeries, loss of function or structural integrity of body secondary to accidents, injury, surgery, congenital disabilities, or paralytic illness

- Environmental exposure, disease, or sensitivity because of toxic metals, mold, or chemicals such as lead and mercury

- Presence of disabilities or poor social and adaptive skills that make one vulnerable to discrimination, rejection, bullying, and trauma

- Substance use problems with drugs of abuse such as opioids, alcohol, stimulants, sedatives, or hallucinogenic substances

- Social factors such as dysfunctional families, friends, or marriages; adverse, toxic, or abusive relationships; divorces; failures in school or work; loss of social support, a significant other, a job or career, a home, or financial security; or a recent move

- Personality issues or chronic adverse personality disorders such as narcissistic, antisocial, dependent, or paranoid personality disorder—which are damaging and disruptive to success and functioning in everyday life activities—leading to the inability to form significant supportive relations

The effects of trauma and its aftermath can occur at any life stage, in childhood or adulthood. The trauma-experience itself can result from a wide variety of situations and predispose to mood disorders like depression. Different types of trauma can affect each person differently and underlie or contribute to trauma-related illness and post-traumatic stress disorder (PTSD).

Contributing traumatic experiences may include:

- Feeling helpless during trauma, as in childhood sexual abuse, rape, physical assault, auto accidents with the threat of injury, violence, or death

- Occurrences of overwhelming, adverse, life-threatening events (early life or in adulthood) or compounded traumas (i.e., series of traumatic events: as a job loss, divorce, death of a significant other, financial loss, subjugation to violence and imprisonment)

- Being a healthcare worker, such as an EMT, nurse, or doctor in medical care work, or a soldier in combat overwhelmed by the witnessing of death and destruction

- Surviving a climatic or natural disaster, a war, a holocaust, a mass casualty event such as a terrorist attack, a pandemic, a mass shooting, or a bombing

- Witnessing domestic violence, death, or injury to others (health care providers, law enforcement, and emergency workers experience much traumatic exposure regularly)

Secondary trauma also happens when witnessing despair and death associated with feeling overwhelmed by their work demands. Look for signs of depression and be ready to provide support and help. After a significant loss or trauma, knowing the mourning stages is critical and helpful to aid someone in need. The grieving and depressed in the COVID-19's wake pandemic need attention, support, and necessary resources.[9]

Be aware of the signs and presentation of depression and severe grief states, especially where there is the progression to major debilitating and life-threatening illnesses. Reach out for help for yourself or someone else in need when a significant loss and death of significant others have occurred. When depression occurs, beyond merely taking an antidepressant pill or a natural remedy, seek the benefits from social support, psychotherapy, and other complementary approaches. Find help from qualified health professionals when needed—preferably those with a more holistic orientation. Learn as much as possible about depression from information, reading, attending educational programs, or support groups.

HOLISTIC

HEALTH STEPS

Coronavirus infections (COVID-19), with their rapid global spread and persistence, cause fear and anxiety. Yet there are steps we can take for prevention and creating more optimal health. The essential steps discussed here apply whether you already have a health compromise, such as from mental or physical illness as lung and airway disease, a weakened immune system, or other chronic illness—or you are in peak health. The right active choices can help prevent and avoid life-threatening forms of an illness or bring quicker recovery. Holistic health steps consider the optimal preparations for the COVID-19 virus, the flu, or other health threats.

Warning signs of infection may appear 2 to 14 days after exposure:

1. Fever
2. Cough
3. Shortness of breath

If these signs appear, get an assessment by a trusted community health resource and move determinedly to make any needed changes. Confirmed coronavirus cases (COVID-19) have ranged from mild symptoms to severe illness and death. *Many already-infected individuals will only have mild upper respiratory symptoms or be asymptomatic carriers of the infection.*

BEING OPTIMALLY FIT

With the COVID-19 virus, many lack any natural immune defense. Unfortunately, those at risk can develop a more severe form of the illness. It is more likely that you would be a non-symptomatic carrier of the infectious agent or experience only mild symptoms by implementing better preparedness. As with any illness, you will have a better chance of survival and recovery as well with adequate preparedness and a consistent health program. The same steps also would be advisable if you already have a compromised immune system or any other existing disease.

Until wide access is available to vaccines that prevent COVID-19 and its variants, the best recommendation is to avoid situations where you may be exposed to those carrying or actively sick with this highly contagious virus. Take preventive actions to help prevent the spread of coronavirus respiratory diseases by following the recommendations from the U.S. Centers for Disease Control and Prevention (CDC).[10]

- Wash your hands with soap and water for at least 20 seconds or use alcohol-based hand rubs covering all surfaces of your hands and rub them together until they feel dry, or use hand sanitizers.
- Cover your mouth and nose with a tissue when coughing or sneezing, and sanitize hands afterward.
- Do not touch your eyes, nose, or mouth with your hands.
- Clean your phone, computers, and other frequently touched areas with sanitizers or disinfection agents.
- Wipe down or spray any possible virus-contaminated surfaces with sanitizers.
- Limit unnecessary social interactions in the community where there are groups of people, particularly indoors or in poorly ventilated areas.

- Maintain social distance between yourself and others by at least six feet when possible.

- Avoid close contact with anyone showing symptoms of respiratory illness such as coughing and sneezing.

- Stay home if you are sick, and stay away from people who are sick.

- Always wear a face mask and correctly socially distance where there is a possibility of close contact with a potential carrier of the virus, even if in an outdoor setting.

ACHIEVING BETTER HEALTH AND PROTECTION

We can choose a more comprehensive and holistic program rather than a too narrow or conventionally focused health improvement plan. Exploring complementary or alternative options may add depth to preparedness and health enhancement. One such option is lifestyle medicine.

"Lifestyle medicine" is a new specialty field joining the prior growing holistic, integrative medicine, and psychiatry fields. Like its predecessors, this field recognizes evidence-based practices that help individuals to adopt and to sustain healthy behaviors. As with holistic and integrative healthcare, the focus is on the root causes of disease, such as an unhealthy diet, limited exercise, poor sleep, and high stress, which affect health and quality of life. Areas of concern are all areas that may affect health and well-being, such as nutrition, exercise, tobacco cessation, stress management, sleep, relationships, and mental health. Interventions in these areas are the priority over medications and procedures whenever alternatives are possible.

More than 70 percent of chronic diseases appear related to adverse lifestyle choices; such diseases also drive up healthcare costs. Those patients who benefit most from a lifestyle-focused treatment plan are those with *early-stage* degenerative illness such as dementia, heart disease, Parkinson's disease, or conditions such as cancer, autoimmune disorders, arthritis, or anxiety and mood disorders. For example, cardiovascular disease, a leading cause of death in the United States, can be prevented most times if obesity, diabetes, hypertension, blood lipids imbalances, and tobacco abuse are reduced or eliminated by lifestyle changes and interventions.[11]

A more holistic and integrative program's general goals would be to regain more optimal health, fitness, well-being and to optimize the body's defenses against any dangerous infection or illness. Without building well-being, one's current level of resistance and the overall state of one's health cannot protect against a potentially life-threatening virus such as the COVID-19 or other unexpected illness.

TIPS: STRATEGIES AND INTERVENTIONS TO CONSIDER

Awareness and support of the mind, body, and spiritual dimensions are essential for wellness, healing, and illness prevention.

- Get the support and any services required for the design of an optimal health program for you. Outside of your usual support networks is a host of resources that may be the key to improving your current health and preparedness level, if you search for them (resources are also presented in this book). Any significant changes you can make now can go a long way to reduce the severity of problems resulting from an infectious exposure or actual illness.

- Be proactive, as the steps presented here may be life-enhancing and life-sustaining.

- Empower yourself: seek more information (through reliable internet sources, healthcare agencies, or providers) and make choices about your health, especially when there are needs for preventive work, interventions, or treatment of any existing conditions.

- Consult with other healthcare practitioners, especially those with a more holistic and integrative orientation. Embracing an overall healthy lifestyle can help decrease health problems. These consultations can help you to gain the skills and practices for increasing longevity and resistance to pathogens such as viruses that prey on weakened immune defenses or vulnerabilities.

- Consider requesting diagnostic tests (for allergies, anemia, diabetes, heart disease, infection, thyroid disease, hormone deficiencies, respiratory illnesses, autoimmune or inflammatory conditions, or early cancer), nutritional status tests for deficiencies, elimination diets (to aid digestive function), or gastrointestinal testing for digestive problems.

There have been, for centuries, investigations into the use of plant-based medicines. Though there has often been the suggestion of benefits to humans, totally conclusive research has often been lacking to support many of the natural remedies purported to be beneficial (the reasons vary from the age of the remedies to local knowledge and use of such treatments to the lack of interest among research funders). Still, some modern medicines have come out of the formal studies of herbs and botanicals. Suggestion of benefits from using natural agents for other coronaviruses, such as SARS, have appeared in past studies. Also, some human cell lines and animal studies showed inconclusively some benefits.

Testing to validate the beneficial use of natural substances has not yet been done in well-designed human clinical studies of coronavirus treatment. Although some natural remedies have shown benefits for prevention, immune-boosting, or illness severity reduction, there is no current research showing value in treating the novel COVID-19 virus. Therefore, the best advice would be to follow the public health guidelines such as social distancing and wearing masks. Also:

- Look to authoritative information and recommendations if considering natural substances as alternatives. If you do so, purchase from a reputable manufacturer or supplier and at your own risk.

- Do seek guidance from authoritative sources, knowledgeable nutritional—or at least nutritionally aware—healthcare providers. Research to the best of your abilities any recommendations. Consider the merits of any suggestions, including the safety and proven benefit for health enhancements. In-depth information is available on natural and nutritional medicine from many current sources, including one of my former colleagues and mentors, Alan Gaby, MD, who compiled a textbook on nutritional medicine.[12]

- Review information on complementary, holistic, or integrative approaches from *trusted and reliable media outlets* (sources can be found on the internet, local lectures, blog sites, or printed materials such as magazines and journals). Receiving guidance or support from an educational program, knowledgeable friends, family members, a teacher, or a health coach can be valuable.

With the widespread use of natural remedies comes hope that future scientific testing will show efficacy, and that these products can be refined to meet those proven standards.

CHOOSE PROGRAMS WITH A HOLISTIC FOCUS

For the optimal support and care for health, disease prevention, or recovery from illness, select a holistic approach that includes comprehensive evaluation for possible adverse contributors to physical, mental, emotional, spiritual, nutritional, and environmental risk factors. Choosing a narrowly oriented practice, which addresses only a few symptoms or one aspect of the entire person, would not be as helpful or advisable.

Significant problems, whether current or from the past, if unrecognized and unresolved, may interfere with your ability to make progress in any therapy or treatment program. Areas often missed or ignored by healthcare providers that may need attention or interventions are:

- Interpersonal conflicts, such as a recent divorce or failed relationship
- Stress overload
- Lack of skills with planning, organizing, and time management
- Job, career loss, or financial crisis

- A move or loss of a home or housing
- The death of a significant other or loved one
- Auto accidents, surgeries, or hospitalizations for illness or injury
- Past traumas, stress disorder symptoms, or traumatic brain injuries
- Emotional or mental health disturbances such as anxiety, fatigue, or depression
- Drug, alcohol, smoking abuse, or addictions
- Eating disorders, diabetes, and obesity

Discuss such factors with your practitioner and then plan accordingly.

EMBRACE A HEALTHY DIET

To support overall health, we can all make good (or better!) dietary choices, including:

- More whole and plant-based foods
- Organic foods, whenever possible
- Avoid too much processed food, which contains sugar and chemical additives
- Eat plenty of vegetables, beans, whole grains (gluten-free, if there is any suggestion of intolerance), greens, fruits, nuts, healthy fats (such as avocados, olive oil, and fats in nuts and seeds)
- If not vegetarian, when possible, choose organic, free-range chicken or beef, or fish from a natural, unpolluted water source

Also, supplements thought to be potentially beneficial for general health, and immune function are:

- Vitamin D in adequate amounts as 1000 to 6000 IU daily, on an as-needed basis, and as advised by your healthcare provider (some practitioners can do Vitamin D testing to bring serum level of 25 OH D in a range between 50-80 nmol/L)
- Vitamin C, orally, in doses as tolerated and as recommended by your healthcare provider

- Selenium
- Zinc, as oral or lozenge preparation, which potentially helps in defenses against respiratory viruses
- Multivitamin combination products
- Probiotics help establish a normal healthy bowel flora (bacteria), which aids digestion and healthy immunity (the immune system depends on a healthy gut and digestive system)
- Melatonin helps sleep and supports positive TH1 immune response, and therefore, reduces stress. Suggestive use has been with as little as 0.5 mg to 3 mg, 30 minutes before sleep
- Botanicals, mushrooms, and herbals are often recommended for their potential immune and health benefits by practitioners of botanical medicine and naturopathy, either as single agents or combined formulations

When possible, review information or recommendations from an experienced nutritionist, a healthcare provider, or a health coach with nutrition expertise. If purchasing any supplements, look for reputable manufacturers and suppliers. When buying over-the-counter, realize that there is no guarantee that any product will be helpful or beneficial, and that you do so at your own risk. Finally, only use prescription and over-the-counter medications *when needed and recommended by a trusted health care provider.*

EXERCISE IS CRUCIAL

Different types of exercise are encouraged as per individual preferences and abilities. Extensive research on exercise has confirmed its value in reducing risks for significant diseases such as heart disease, hypertension, mood disturbance, cancer, dementia, obesity, diabetes, stress, and sleep-related illnesses. Only exercise to your capacity. If you are unsure where to start, especially when there is any potential for stroke, heart attack, or other potential negative consequences, get an exercise prescription or advice from a healthcare provider or a personal trainer.

A variety of exercises in your program give you the best overall training effect and prevent boredom. Activities that are popular and beneficial are biking, walking, weight training, running, hiking, dancing, aerobic classes, swimming, yoga, qigong, tennis, or other individual or team sports. Any active movement is helpful and worthwhile. There are also calming, stress-reducing, focusing exercises, like meditation and yoga, which can be a fantastic addition to any health and exercise program. Consistent regular exercise can help prevent infections, decrease the illness's length and intensity, and speed recovery.[13]

OPTIMIZE YOUR SLEEP

Poor sleep, insomnia, getting into "sleep debt" or sleep deprivation (not getting enough sleep), or other sleep disturbances are associated with significant medical problems like obesity, diabetes, accidents, shoddy work, hampered school performance, and mood troubles. A good start in improving sleep is to reduce stress, over-stimulation, and activity overload throughout the day, but especially in the evenings and in an hour or two before bedtime.

Do meditative or deep relaxation exercises. Improve your mood, reduce anxiety, and reduce worry—if there are significant mood or anxiety problems, see an appropriate healthcare professional or therapist for assessment and treatment if needed. If a sleep specialist checks out daytime sleepiness or a history of loud snoring, a sleep disorder such as sleep apnea may need to be diagnosed and treated.

ENVIRONMENTAL FACTORS

Environmental factors play a role in health and disease. Allergies, sensitivities, or reactivity to toxic substances and chemicals can impair health or hinder recovery. Pollutants may be present in the air, water, soil, pesticides, or food additives. Toxicity in the environment can include "toxic" or irritating relationships, excessive noise, intrusiveness, or disruptions by others such as in your workplace or where you live.

Other toxic environmental situations may be the lack of a quiet sleep or rest place, excessive electronic or radio-frequency disturbance (TV, radios, cell phones, microwave), or chemical fumes (perfumes, pesticides, industrial chemicals). Currently, there is also concern about the genetic modification of foods (also known as GMOs). Be aware of possible environmental issues in your local area and seek authoritative sources of environmental health information.

THE IMPORTANCE OF SPIRITUALITY

The study, reflection, and application of ideas from the vast world of spiritual and religious philosophies, practices, or faiths can be an essential part of your transformation into more positive states of health, well-being, or recovery from illness. When stuck in states of emotional despair or depression, as when traditional mental health services used alone have not helped, surrounding yourself with supportive, nurturing, and inspiring people can bring about a release from stifling and rigid patterns of personal thoughts and beliefs. Such shifts toward better emotional and spiritual attunement, and adjustment to life's demands and conflicts, often bring better health and well-being. Finding healthy activities that bring joy, purpose, fulfillment, meaning, and gratification can open the spirit's doors and promote wellness.[14]

POSITIVE BRAIN ADAPTIVITY (NEUROPLASTICITY)

Recent findings on brain adaptivity have implications for mental and emotional health issues, such as addiction, depression, anxiety, and post-traumatic stress disorder (PTSD), present many challenges to old ideas about recovery and transformation. Advances in neuroplasticity, neuroscience, and its technology to change brain neuro-circuitry, human behavior, and responses bring new helpful tools. These advances have contributed to improved outcomes in what were previously considered untreatable and chronic disabling conditions. Holistic healing programs, when possible, incorporate these new, validated scientific methods into treatment protocols.

Any person involved in recovery and transformative work must first accept the disease as an integral part of their everyday life experience. The realization that healing and recovery require profound personal change must also be present. However, pursuing treatment on a superficial level is often the case. For example, in substance use disorders, or any other persistent or disabling illness, this surface approach often fails. And those failures often occur because of factors such as making a limited commitment to meaningful changes in personal attitudes; learned habits; or placing too much expectation that prior reliance upon personal resources, medication, or other supports will help.

PSYCHONEUROPLASTICITY (PNP)

Presented in *Psychoneuroplasticity Protocols for Addictions* (Lawlis et al., 2015) is evidence-based science with restorative, rehabilitative, and transformational tools and applications. Developments in neuroscience, neural therapies, rehabilitation medicine, addiction, and other integrative approaches to mental health treatments contributed to psychoneuroplasticity's (PNP's) development. Though the book focuses on evidence-based treatment approaches for addiction, these apply to other mental health issues and problems that respond to integrative approaches and therapies. Brain plasticity expresses the brain's neuronal circuitry, responses to stimulation, ability to change nerve cells, and other complex networks.[15]

Positive brain plasticity can be helpful in addressing:

- Cognitive processing, physical pain, and migraines
- Emotions, depression, anger, reactiveness, and stress
- Anxiety, fear, phobias, obsessiveness, and distractibility
- Alertness, focus, arousal, ADHD, brain fog, and fatigue
- PTSD, sleep disturbance, addictions, cravings, and being over-weight

To set the stage for healing, recovery, transformation, and neuroplasticity, other difficulties, as noted below, may need attention to benefit from PNP.

ANXIETY AND FEAR

As discussed in detail in an earlier chapter, anxiety and fear can be disabling conditions and can interfere with life and productivity. They can also become a barrier to recovery from other mental or physical health conditions. Recall that the following can contribute to anxiety or panic-like disorders:

- Unmanaged stress
- Prior life losses and trauma

- Lack of adequate parenting or an early life-nurturing environment
- Adverse effects of medication and drugs
- Life-threatening physical illness

The resulting impairment can become chronic, with only temporary relief from prescription drugs or the use of unregulated substances that could be harmful to one's health and well-being.

When such conditions are present, studies of brain waves often will show high-frequency beta waves in localized regions of the brain, suggesting increased activation and the need to retrain and repair the brain's neural networks to more relaxed frequencies and a healthier state. Mental health professionals sometimes labeled people as having other mental health conditions as personality disorders, because they could not grow and mature emotionally. In reality, the persistent behaviors and "personality disorders" can be related to earlier abuse, persistent severe anxiety, and feelings of being overwhelmed—all of which affect brain function. This can result in resistance or the inability to resolve the tension that blocks healthy development around families, social networks, and peers.

TRAUMATIC LIFE EVENTS

Traumatic events can lead to post-traumatic stress disorder (PTSD), which can either be of a simple type (where there has only been one significant traumatic event) or complex (where there have been multiple, cumulative traumas). A person's life development can get stuck in a time relation to that earlier trauma. Integrative-type treatment protocols and therapies focusing on trauma treatment can relieve the emotional connection to traumatic memories and support positive brain plasticity changes.

To counteract this damage, neurofeedback treatments, as with the BAUD (bio-acoustical utilization device), disrupt the reconsolidation of traumatic memory, which can relieve PTSD symptoms in some patients. Relaxation or stress-reducing therapies, music, meditation practices, breathing techniques, nutritious diet, and neuro-biofeedback can be a part of neuroplasticity enhancing protocols. Other sensory or trauma-focused treatments, such as EMDR, can help to form new and healthy neuro-circuitry and response patterns.

DEPRESSION

As we know, depression can interfere with recovery due to a multitude of factors, including:

- Response to adverse life events, chronic stress, trauma, and losses
- Low self-esteem
- Genetics, nutritional deficiencies, and medical illness
- Toxic environmental exposure including drugs and alcohol

With depression, there may be associated features such as ruminations and obsessional thoughts, as seen in obsessive compulsive disorder (OCD); anxiety; loss of productivity; feelings of loss of control; loss of interest in favorite activities and things; or a downward spiral of increasing depression and development of suicidal thinking, which can lead to loss of life or complication with other medical illness. If suicidal thinking occurs, find immediate help from a mental health professional.

If a person with depression has EEG-brain wave studies, the brain will often show a pattern of underactivation and low-voltage waves. Neuroplasticity-focused protocols then look for health interventions to bring these areas of the nervous system back online and to restore responsive feelings, energy, joy, and happiness, without the individual resorting to using potentially dangerous drugs or chemicals. Intervention may use therapies including:

- Neurofeedback or neuro-therapies and the BAUD
- Psychotherapies including trauma-focused treatments, such as EMDR
- Exercise, nutritional diet, and supplements
- Sound, rhythm, aroma, movement, and dance therapy
- Mindful meditation and breathing techniques

- Social network development with active peer support
- Coping, relapse prevention, and social skill development

Cyclic patterns of disturbed emotions and behaviors can also interfere with recovery. Problematic patterns of feelings or behaviors of concern could be excessive irritability, rage, heightened anxiety, obsessiveness, sleep disturbance, periods of a dramatic increase in activity, hyper-focus alternating with fatigue, depression, loss of motivation, and loss of interest in things. These patterns are sometimes labeled as being in the bipolar spectrum but can also be related to PTSD and prior accumulative trauma. Integrative, holistic, or neuroplasticity approaches can help.

BEYOND EGO, PERSONALITY, HABITS, AND BEHAVIORS

To the person afflicted, life can become unmanageable, with feelings of hopelessness, helplessness, and powerlessness. The only way out is to surrender the old established self-survival practices, beliefs, and dependencies and to realize the potential of being a part of something more extensive, with greater power and opportunity for transformation and change.

Repeated failures or relapses in illness or recovery work may be because of:

- Non-effective coping strategies, actions, or efforts to feel sufficient, empowered, and adequate
- Manipulation and other tactics to control external obstacles and people
- Efforts to rebuild failing relationships, in order to fulfill unmet needs for nurturance, love, and acceptance

After running out of the "customary" choices for getting by, especially when there have been setbacks and threats to survival, a willingness occurs to let go of the old and embrace options from a larger pool of opportunities or possibilities. One realizes the limitations of a solitary person's competence, power, and ability to change. The power of a more significant source of hope, possibilities, and options opens as a window of new light and promise for the individual drowning in frustration and survival fears.

Gaining flexibility and the freedom to explore and invest in behaviors or practices favorable to recovery and transformation include getting unstuck from rigid behaviors, beliefs, and self-concepts; this means shifting from unproductive ideas about power and control—perhaps a product of development and programming since birth—and realizing that there is a tremendous potentiality, a higher resource beyond an individual's limitations and beliefs. Such programming can include deeply held core beliefs about one's self and are a barrier to change, such as:

1. Not being safe
2. Not being loved
3. Not being enough
4. Not being worthy (as when burdened with guilt and shame)

When a person arrives at a place of great despair, a sort of "dark night of the soul," a critical time comes, ushering in the need to let go of the established, limiting "ego identity." Embracing spiritual attunement becomes a viable option. That time that is fertile for accepting personal limitations; an openness to greater possibilities and potentialities prevails, where love, acceptance, and inclusiveness are paramount. Embracing the essence of being awake and fully present allows for empowerment and motivation for the steps required for transformation, such as the restoration of "sanity" as identified in the second of *The Twelve Steps* of Alcoholics Anonymous and other 12-step programs.

SPIRITUAL EMERGENCE

Spirituality unfolds with the experience of personal awakening, beyond the constriction and restriction set by the learned and programmed mind-ego. A higher level of perception, realization, and functioning occurs with transient or sometimes longer-lasting change. In Asheville, NC, the Center for Spiritual Emergence describes spiritual emergence as a "natural opening and awakening that many people experience as a result of coming to terms with the difficulties of life, through an established faith tradition, as a result of systematic spiritual practices or through unexpected peak experiences. Spiritual emergences gently allow one to experience and embrace their natural connection to the transcendent domain, forever changing their limiting self concepts into a more integrative, awakened self."[16]

MEDITATION, A MENTAL HEALTH ESSENTIAL

MEDITATION, MINDFULNESS, OR INTROSPECTIVE PRACTICES

Disciplines that encourage us to slow down and reflect have proven their value in holistic mental health approaches for mood disorders, anxiety, addictions, and other health issues. **Some form of meditation can be an essential tool for happiness and well-being.** Enhancement of longevity and a decrease in brain aging are beneficial in other areas of life (which may also include work, school, and athletic performance; sleep quality; and creativity). The mere awareness in meditation that thoughts and emotions are of a changing and transient nature is enlightening for those imprisoned by harsh, negative thoughts and feelings.

Twenty-five-hundred or more years of practice and study of introspection and meditation practices by yogis, Buddhists, mystics of all religions, philosophers, academics, psychologists, and scientists, in thousands of research papers, seem to confirm the value of meditation. People have never found that temporarily resolving conflicts or problems, or seeking pleasure or gratification has ever brought any lasting happiness, contentment, or relief from suffering. In people prone to conflict, resolving an interpersonal issue may lead to a temporary feeling of security, peacefulness, or happiness. However, this can pass quickly when new areas of conflict or insecurity arise, and results—again and again—in pain, suffering, and unhappiness. With the practice of introspection, meditation, or self-reflection, there is an uncovering, unveiling, or revelation of the always-present, ever-existent peacefulness, serenity, happiness, and harmony in the core of our natural being.

A PROMISE OF MENTAL HEALTH

By taking constructive action, happiness and improved mental health can follow. Being more attuned with nature allows for an unperturbed mind, stress and conflict resolution, and gratification from rewarding and fulfilling activities. The potential for happiness was always present, but was perhaps hidden by the mind's restless activity. Our clarity and personal experience, then, come from our mind's ability to focus, allowing for a clearer perception of objects, thoughts or movement to an infinite array of other inputs.

On the other hand, hyper-focusing of mental activity or obsessing can obscure the awareness of more extensive perceptual experiences. Many names are given to the broader nature of things or the undefined source: the Unknowable, all that is beyond the mind's grasp, the Spirit, the ground of all experience, the Infinite, a timeless origin of all our experience of being, G-d, Brahma, Allah, and so on, depending on one's concepts, culture, or education. Quantum physicists might even name this as "infinite undefinable space" or use other scientific terms.

The tightness—finite focusing—of mind towards rigid ideas, concepts, beliefs, insecurities, and fears relaxes and lightens up with meditation. The gradual awakening of spirit and the experiencing of the always-present happiness and peacefulness unfold.

Similarly, going from the waking state into dream sleep, we transcend into a less contracted mind and mental activity focus. There is a looser array of objects making up a dream story, one that can be happy, peaceful, or fearful if there is a carry-over of stressful, negative emotions from the awake state. The final falling into a deep sleep is usually restful and peaceful—some, however, remain on high alert, never getting into much deep sleep, rejuvenating, or recovering for the next day of wakefulness and focused mental activity.

The art of meditation is a simple movement or release away from mental activity such as thoughts, thinking, planning, conceptualizing, worrying, obsessing, fantasizing, imaging, daydreaming, etc. An idea or thought-like action may be rigid, constricted, fearful, panicky, open, mindful, relaxed, accepting, or flexible. Another way of explaining meditation would be the release from a state of tightness, anxiety, fear, and vulnerability; to a place of relaxation, letting go, and openness, for the experiencing of states of peacefulness, openness, well-being, and happiness. Meditation enhances happiness and peacefulness as a personal benefit and also carries over to other relationships. Developing awareness beyond the mind's usual narrow focus encourages empathy, respect, and compassion for all outside of our everyday personal experience.

THE LINK TO NEUROPLASTICITY

Regular practices are essential to gain a training effect and positive brain change. Reduction of stress hormones and overactivity of the brain's emotional regulation areas (such as the amygdala) occur with meditation. Practices can be with the intention of self-benefit but also for the betterment of all. Reduction and relief from mood disorders, fearful and emotional states, and post-trauma symptoms can improve with awareness and meditation practices. Prevention of relapses from illness or addiction happens by regular meditation-related releases from a busy mind, anxiety, and stress.

WHERE TO START, OR HOW TO IMPROVE PRACTICES

The often-busy mind will mask the greater awareness or context of experience. If you look at a piece of art and get lost in one object in the picture, you won't appreciate the image in its entirety. If you're driving a car and become distracted by looking for a street sign, you risk hitting the vehicle in front of you. If you watch a movie and get too focused on one character in the film, you lose the sense of what the entire picture was about (the context). You might even forget that it was just a constructed moving picture story projected on an initially empty screen.

Being aware of awareness is a fundamental task in self-reflection, meditation, and mindfulness. One need not master yoga postures, recite esoteric mantras, sit in any unique way, be in a particular setting or class, or breathe in any special manner. Many practices and teachings may help advance your learning and training, especially if any of the offerings catch your fancy. Bring meditation, self-reflection, and mindfulness into as much of your daily living as possible, whenever you remember and are able. Be mindful when you are moving or still, when you are breathing, exercising, interacting with another, talking, or listening—in any time, place, or situation. As an example, if you are walking, you can do a brief walking mindfulness meditation.

If you are a beginner, consider any of the resources recommended in this book, or seek informative reading, or even a class. Remember that staying tuned to the bigger picture is essential. Also essential are awareness and mindfulness as you live, breathe, and go about your daily living and activities. Practice just being aware and present and remain as the subjective observer as you move through your day. Allow all the sensory and mental images, thoughts, and objects to exist in their natural state of constant change and movement through your awareness.

AWARENESS, A KEY TO
RECOVERY AND HEALING

"Why do you stay in prison when the door is wide open?"

- Rumi (Sufi poet and mystic)

Awareness, essential for healing, defines the attentiveness and appreciation of experience, including everything beyond our usual perceptions, knowledge, and biases. Developing awareness is a vital step for recovering from disease and illness. Centuries ago, the Buddha realized the link between suffering and attachment. He proposed that, in sickness, the mind holds tightly to a narrowed set of thoughts, interpretations, and feelings. The repetitive focus leads to entrapment in mental activity during a health-threatening condition. Meditation was one way the Buddha recommended breaking this entrapment. The mind attaches naturally to any perceived threat and gives attention to what the body might need. However, for healing to occur, there needs to be a shift towards greater awareness and openness for alternative solutions, positive health behaviors, adaptations, and skill development.

Someone who has chronic pain, addictions, depression, cancer, or life-threatening illness experiences different suffering levels during the disease. Because of an adverse condition, the person may find themselves locked into thoughts about the threat to their lives and well-being. Fears may develop regarding future difficulties. An individual may worry about death, losing function, or the capacity to work or care for oneself or others. An essential aspect of the healer's work, then, is to provide help, a listening presence, wise guidance, and education. Also needed is sharing techniques that facilitate the release from unhealthy attachment, especially to rigid ideas, concepts, and unproductive worries. The hope is to help alleviate pain and suffering, and to enhance healing and wellness.

FOUNDATION OF THE HEALING ARTS

The healing arts have adopted fundamental ideas derived from schools of spiritual philosophy, psychology, and religion. Basics include the value of bringing awareness to the mind's activity, which helps both healer and sufferer. Each wisdom tradition has concepts related to:

- The care and nurture of the body, mind, and spirit
- The achievement of greater happiness
- The gaining of freedom from the bondage or entrapment in a shallow, unenlightened world of a limiting and inflexible self-ego

With development and practice, the division of self-ego and the spiritual awareness melt away into an experience of oneness and unity.

ILLNESS AND AWARENESS

With illness or severe loss, the developed self-concept of one's world strengthens but also becomes limiting. This developed self-ego has locked-in ideas of what novel experiences mean in terms of rewards, nourishment, or threat. Depending on the learning, parenting, and earlier life experiences, the self-ego gets imprinted with adaptive or maladaptive learned patterns, reactive thoughts, judgments, concepts, images, and responses. After trauma, thoughts and reactions may also be maladaptive, decreasing flexibility to adapt to changing circumstances, perpetuating pain and adversity.

As a result, the person then becomes *less adaptable* and feels more vulnerable, which intensifies fear and suffering. The degree of fearfulness depends on the level of held inflexibility. With greater rigidity comes a lessened ability to adapt, to change, to heal, or transform. Yet, an opportunity always exists to move towards openness, acceptance, flexibility, spiritual growth, and well-being.

The quest for a path to liberation from a rigid or limiting personal experience has been a significant challenge for most. Attempts to define or describe the undefinable or "felt sense" of something greater or beyond our limited selves have led to confusion. Many related concepts or terms, adding difficulty, came from diverse fields such as science, spirituality, religion, and mysticism.

Being stuck in fixed behaviors or patterns may be part of the actual cause of perpetuated or chronic illness. The ability to be flexible and make changes contributes to healing. If caught in a limiting self-ego, a clouded state of awareness with loss of spiritual insight, help is possible through seeking inspiring experiences, guidance, training, or fellowship with individuals, social networks, groups, or organizations offering support and services.

Most such schools of spiritual development teach the importance of following a regular practice. Gradual movement is encouraged—from rational thoughts, feelings, emotions, and body awareness, to the freeing experience of profound silence, serenity, and well-being—as in prayer, meditation, or contemplation. The release into the peace of "open awareness" goes beyond the usual mental activity of interpretation and judgment.

The progression to what is sometimes called "enlightenment" often follows a gradual awakening of awareness and acceptance of change and impermanence. The experience of an enlightened consciousness can either happen as a sudden shift, a mere glimpse, or may occur after some catastrophic event or bout of severe suffering. Holistic and non-dual therapies support and nurture the development of a healthier yet flexible sense of self, awareness, and interconnectedness with all life as part of the healing process.

Awareness, openness, acceptance, and flexibility contribute to better life adaptation, recovery, and healing. Gaining freedom from mental or physical suffering and attachments are aided by:

- Realization of the healing space, which may be beyond one's contrived, self-limiting notions and beliefs
- Getting beyond personal rigid fixed ideas, concepts, and beliefs
- Allowing for movement and release from repetitive thoughts, actions, and behaviors
- Developing an openness to a sense of more possibilities, flexibility, fearlessness, peacefulness, and serenity

In a medical context, the goal is to promote better functioning and adaptability to everyday life stresses, enhance individual growth, and develop beyond an over-limiting personal self and behavior patterns.

THE "SECRET" TO HEALTH AND WELL-BEING

Everyone searches for answers to health and well-being, but few find them. To uncover the **"SECRET"** to health, we can begin a healthy process of removing accumulated harmful emotional debris, layers of unhelpful ideas, and limiting concepts. Open your mind to being «health-wise.»

S = Spirituality, Serenity, Surrender

Find peace by letting go and accepting things as they are. Understand and acknowledge that you pay a high price for the added burdens, worries, and stress you carry. Surrender the unnecessary and non-essentials. Release the unneeded to experience greater awareness and connection with the truth beyond your knowledge, biased interpretations, and perceptions.

E = Experience life with open awareness, letting go of entrapment from personal conditioning, words, concepts, and memories

C = Compassion, Calmness, and Completeness

Allow acceptance, rather than the attitude of *lack* or the belief that you need to be something more than you are. Find resolutions for any anxieties or fears of being vulnerable or incomplete.

R = Renewal, Regeneration, and the Regaining of the connection with your inner being, the true self, to heal your mind, body, and spirit

Unleash the vital energy held captive by the chains of stress. Gain freedom by letting go of the constant struggle to maintain a more-than-needed, "protective identity": what developed from memories and a "felt need" to be safe, meaningful, influential, purposeful, and adequate.

E = Enlightenment and Experiencing an open awareness by being in the presenting moment

Allow release from the constraints of over-identification with being a separate self (an "ego"), allowing entry into the broader healing context from the wounds of separation and alienation. Many teachers and sages emphasize the experience or experiential learning that comes through practices, participation, and community support.

T = Transpersonal, experiencing connectedness to all life—beyond your personality, beliefs, education, and culture—is being in the health and healing zone.

TIPS: AWARENESS

Some practices to consider for integrative healing and growth that support balanced development of a healthy body, mind, and spirit include:

- Non-dual oriented therapies
- Active, consistent exercise, along with a balanced program of rest and recreation
- Yoga, chi gong, and meditation
- Spiritual practices from either one's background or other religious or spiritual traditions

- Addiction and substance abuse treatment (if needed)
- Reducing exposure to harmful environmental toxins and allergens
- Correction of medical, metabolic, or hormone issues
- Following a more nutritious, organic, plant-based diet with correction of deficiencies through vitamins, minerals, and essential fatty acids; and health enhancement with herbs and botanicals
- Massage, acupuncture, deep relaxation, and other body-based therapies
- "Other-serving," such as volunteer and community service work; charitable and compassionate help to others in need; caring for a pet
- Communing with nature and caring for the environment

When pursuing awareness, study with a *credible, experienced, trustworthy* non-dual therapist, a spiritual teacher, or a mentor when the opportunity presents itself. Read and explore, individually or in groups, the great spiritual teachers' writings and teachings and other philosophies and traditions. Be compassionately present. Be who you are, fully aware, liberated, and open to all existing potentialities, not a "who" constricted by limiting mind programming, learning, or sets of reactivity.[17]

WHEN IT IS ALL PERSONAL

In the months before the onset of COVID-19 cases in our country and local area, my wife had a fainting spell, with a hard fall and injury to her hip, requiring an ER visit. She had a recurrence of heart arrhythmias, called atrial fibrillation, which she had suffered in the past. In the ER, her hip was x-rayed and was not fractured, but the heart was in a dangerous and rapid irregular rhythm. A cardiologist wasn't immediately available, and for several hours, attempts continued with the ER doctor trying to correct her heart rhythm, including painful infusions of anti-arrhythmia medication and electro-conversion attempts with electric shocks. Finally, a cardiologist came and recommended a different course of treatment with medication.

Over several days, she converted back to a regular heart rate and rhythm. A planned corrective ablation procedure kept her on the cardiology unit. The process required anesthesia and an inserted cardiac catheter that treated the problem area. She was held on the intensive monitoring unit for several days, waiting for the ablation procedure. She fasted overnight on two different days, only to find out she was off the surgery schedule, as patients with more serious illness needed the specialist's services. Along with the stress of waiting for the heart procedure, she experienced mounting anxiety over hip pain and an inability to walk from the fall. Though a physical therapist finally helped, the orthopedic doctor never arrived for consultation.

After four days on the cardiac unit, a heart specialist saw her and determined that she didn't need a procedure because, by that time, she was exhausted, highly anxious, and her heart was back to a normal rhythm with medications. She was discharged home after the experience of this whole fear-inducing and traumatic ordeal.

In the past, she had other frightening experiences of blacking out, along with terrorizing episodes of heart arrhythmias. These episodes had been put at bay for several years after successful open-heart surgery to replace a congenitally defective heart valve. Yet the medications that began in the hospital had caused uncomfortable side effects. In addition, the cardiologist's follow-up visits had been brief, with minimal concern about the level of anxiety and worries. With palpitations continuing, the possibility of having an elective ablation heart procedure was raised. I couldn't fully come to grips with the level of impersonal care and with what I had witnessed and experienced during my wife's hospitalization.

FACING CHALLENGES POSED BY COVID-19

With healthcare changing towards specialization and large corporate medical groups, I had always advocated for holistic and integrative health care. With our recent healthcare misadventure, I was still disappointed and dismayed at the full reality of the changes affecting ourselves personally and of other people's healthcare. My wife and I had many talks about our experience, but even with our best attempts to understand and accept things, there remained a high level of lingering fear and foreboding that more was to come.

Some friends had gone on a long-awaited cruise ship vacation when the first cases of COVID-19 appeared. They felt assured that they would be safe, but both returned with infections and were then hospitalized with COVID-19. The more at-risk member had to go on a ventilator and died after a valiant struggle. The surviving spouse gradually recovered and returned home to deal with the painful grief and loss.

By that time, COVID-19 had become a pandemic. My wife and I became more fearful of what would happen if there was a recurrence of a life-threatening heart irregularity and the need for hospitalization during the pandemic spreading to our region. A 30-day heart monitoring was done and showed some recurrence of atrial fibrillation. We called a respected heart rhythm specialist at a university medical center in a neighboring state. Going there, about a six-hour drive from our home, was recommended, so that she could receive a preventive and corrective heart procedure. We outfitted ourselves with the best protective gear and packed enough food so we could eat on the road. We stayed the days needed at a hotel recommended by the hospital, with extraordinary precautions for COVID-19 prevention. We could also get all our meals through room service. Our fears about the trip and the dangers of getting infected rapidly subsided as we rested in the hotel.

Then, a major stressful event occurred. We had to go out in a rainstorm to the hospital outpatient lab in order to have a required COVID-19 test two days before entering the hospital. The lab was on the other side of town. Directions were inadequate, and our GPS device malfunctioned. We got lost and were in a bit of a panic, but we finally found the lab at the last minute. There was a long line of cars with people waiting to get tested. We just barely made it before the lab closed and in time to make it to the bathrooms. We were both frazzled when we got back to our lodging and collapsed into a restful sleep. We got a call later that tests were negative.

We reported to the university medical center hospital's cardiac procedure area for the corrective cardiac ablation with the negative COVID-19 test. Each report, as I was waiting, was that everything was fine with excellent progress. The procedure took more than six hours.

A week after our return home, though neither of us caught COVID-19, my wife developed severe spasmodic headaches on the same side of the head and neck where she had the catheterization procedure. The headaches turned out to be a severe case of shingles, felt to be related to the stress of the prior two months. A week after getting shingles treatment, she developed a drug rash all over her body. My wife had to stop all medications.

The post-ablation four-month follow-up took place with the cardiology nurse practitioner. And as my wife had a return of palpitations several times per day, the nurse practitioner ordered a month-long portable heart monitor to determine the need for a blood thinner or other heart medication. It was an appropriate recommendation, but with a narrow look at the complete picture; anxiety itself may have contributed to the palpitations and underlying distress.

The presence of worry, anxiety dreams, and more irritability than usual suggested some post-traumatic stress signs. Of course, watching too much news of the current tumultuous political turmoil probably didn't help. The fear of getting another significant heart arrhythmia most likely added fuel to the body's stress response. The need to go back on previously poorly tolerated medications or rehospitalization was another concern.

My wife also had an increased level of fear and mistrust of medical services with her experience of less personalized holistic care and attentive listening. A little more time and attention could have allowed for a better in-depth understanding of the issues involved with the recurrence of her cardiac events. However, the test went well with a return to heart health. Life was almost back to normal except for the continuing threat of COVID-19 and the wait for the vaccine. The return to heart health and over-all well-being and fitness occurred in parts from medical and cardiology care and her lifelong adherence to an active health program that emphasized nutrition, exercise, and a holistic-oriented lifestyle.

Our personal experience during the COVID-19 pandemic highlights the trauma, crises, mental health challenges, stress, and calamities that affect us all in different ways. The common occurrence of challenging times and experiences reflects the need for better access and more programs with integrative and holistic approaches. Another poignant point is about personal healthcare responsibility, namely, the need for awareness and active steps to learn about ways to improve emotional, spiritual, and physical health with positive actions and choices.

The difficulties of my scenario with the hospitals and healthcare systems' service delivery reflect, I believe, the experience of many in our society, including:

- A developing system with more reliance on advanced technologies
- Growing dependence on a business model with an emphasis on economy of scale (that is, a proportionate saving in costs gained by an increased level of production)
- The perceived need to deliver medical care to larger numbers of people with reduced expenses, increased workload per provider, and hiring less costly personnel
- Less use of psychosocial and mental health services
- Use of fewer trained paraprofessionals and health aides to address patient care needs
- Reduced attention to each individual's unique needs, differences, and critical underlying issues

Much work remains to reduce the disparities in the disadvantaged, lower-income population. There needs to be increased healthcare resources available to all in our society, especially those who are underprivileged or living in communities with economic disadvantages and inadequate healthcare resources.

Awareness and change can occur to develop more advanced and holistic modeling for better and more humanistic healthcare to all in need. There can be improved application and utilization of the positive advances in developing technology, such as telemedicine, and more innovative medical care practice modeling in smaller delivery entities, such as clinics, and more extensive programs through hospitals and public health organizations.

I can envision and reimagine our healthcare system changed and remodeled into integrative programs with a diversified healthcare service provider team. All training programs for healthcare providers, including physicians, need to have holistic and integrative care training. Larger multi-specialty and service centers would have one centralized location, with smaller modules located strategically for all in need. Ideally, the larger centralized centers would include:

- Services with both generalists and specialists, psychosocial services (psychiatrists, sociologists, psychologists, addiction specialists, social workers), and somatic services (family medicine practitioners, generalists, internists, medical specialists, wellness and lifestyle medicine specialists, physical therapists, nutritionists, exercise physiologists)
- Spiritual services (clergy, mindfulness, yoga meditation teachers, spiritual emergence guides)
- Educational in-service for staff training, and educational activity for all participants and community, with programs in person, virtually, and through social media
- Therapists and educators in the areas of movement and exercise, recreational activities, cooking and nutrition, art, vocational rehabilitation, occupational therapy, and narrative healthcare

In the past, programs developed with these intentions included Kaiser Permanente and other health maintenance organizations (HMO). Kaiser Permanente has been one of the few to do well and survive. When I worked for several HMOs early in my career, including Kaiser, there was always a struggle to make the business and cost side of these healthcare plans successful, and many failed. In recent years, working in the public health sector and well-designed addiction treatment programs, I have seen progress in developing integrative and holistic models. In my community practice years, I tried as much as possible to be an exemplary individual integrative and holistic practitioner. I relied heavily, however, on an extended network of holistic and integrative oriented practitioners.

Now, there must be careful study and recommendations from existing and prior HMO-like programs to develop and improve healthcare models for local, statewide, and national needs. Support and research from academic institutions, universities, large hospital systems, and task forces at the state and federal levels would be essential. The funding and investment would hopefully come from governmental, private, and charitable philanthropic sources.

POST-SCRIPT

One last note: the original cardiologist who took care of my wife at the sizeable local cardiology practice group was interested and moving toward holistic and integrative healthcare. He did his best under the time constraints and pressure of the large, corporate business model of the group that employed him. I remember that he was a marathon runner. He finally left the large group and was the first physician to get certified in the new Lifestyle Medicine specialty board. I hope that my wife and I positively influenced him—when we weren't complaining, of course![18]

.

PART II: COPING WITH MENTAL HEALTH ISSUES

A HOLISTIC APPROACH TO SURVIVING BIPOLAR ILLNESS

Ben* was on several medications from his psychiatrist after returning from a psychiatric hospitalization for his bipolar disorder and suicide attempt with pills. Before that, he had progressively worsening depression, feelings of hopelessness, helplessness, and loss of interest in almost everything. He felt frustrated that his mood-cycling illness was only getting worse—even with all his medications. The medications made him feel like a "zombie." He was sleeping less, with frequent violent nightmares that woke him multiple times during the night. He had periods of severely depressed mood, causing him to stay in bed most of the day. Ben would have some days of feeling relatively okay. He then would experience periods of feeling "super hyped-up," full of energy with little need for sleep, talkative with racing thoughts, craving sex and food all the time, feeling like he was a famous rock star, and spending vast amounts of money on things he didn't need. He had lost all of his recent jobs and was now divorced from his second wife.

Ben's family encouraged him to see a holistic, integrative health care practitioner and therapist besides his regular psychiatrist. Ben revealed a significant alcohol problem to his new therapist, as well as his mother's bipolar illness and alcoholism history. His holistic doctor and therapist detected substantial childhood trauma, post-traumatic stress symptoms, digestive problems from gluten intolerance, and autoimmune thyroid disease with a thyroid imbalance.

Ben began specific treatment and therapy programs for his bipolar illness, trauma history, alcoholism, nutritional problems, and thyroid disease. He then worked more closely with his regular psychiatrist, who could eliminate unnecessary medications for the first time. He slept better, with less mood cycling. His new therapy work also helped him to identify and work through some painful childhood issues. Ben regained his pleasure and spiritual connection to things of value.

(*To protect confidentiality, the above is a composite of some clinical experiences and does not represent an actual person or any prior patients).

WHAT CAUSES BIPOLAR ILLNESS, AND WHO IS AFFECTED?

Bipolar illness (BPI), often referred to as bipolar disorder or manic depression, affects over 2.2 million people in the United States. BPI presents with bouts of illness with significant, often disabling symptoms, alternating with periods of less or no symptoms. Signs of the disorder may include unusual shifts in mood, energy, or the ability to function. A significant increase in BPI-related mental illness problems can be anticipated during any crisis times, as seen with the COVID-19 pandemic.

Bipolar illness appears, according to research studies, to have a genetic and inherited basis that causes an instability in the regulation of brain neurotransmitters (nerve chemicals). As a result, a person has greater vulnerability to emotional or physical stress, overstimulation, upsetting life experiences, drug or alcohol use, and interference with rest and sleep. The brain cannot correctly calm or activate itself or restore its usual healthy balance.

First-degree relatives of people with BPI are seven times more likely to develop Bipolar I type of BPI. Environmental factors (epigenetic factors) are also suspected to affect bipolar illness, such as radiation exposure, physical or psychological trauma, chemicals, pesticides, toxic metals, air pollution, bacteria, mold, and viruses.

Lifetime prevalence estimates are 1% for Bipolar I disorder (BP 1), 1.1% for Bipolar II disorder (BP 2), and 2.4% to 4.7% for sub-threshold BPI (a person is not meeting the full symptom criteria for BP 1 or BP 2). The age of onset ranges from childhood to the mid-20s and later, and BPI onset is unusual after 40. Recurrence of active BPI over five years is widespread, with the associated in-between times of no symptoms, minor symptoms, or significant residual symptoms.[19]

EACH INDIVIDUAL HAS UNIQUE TREATMENT NEEDS

Any individual who has difficulties with mood changes is unique regarding their treatment needs. Factors that influence BPI can include:

- Background and neurodiversity (inherited genetic uniqueness and traits)
- Earlier life experiences, exposures, or trauma
- Current lifestyle, nutrition, environment
- Individual medical issues
- Adverse personality issues
- Psychological or addiction issues
- Traumatic brain injury or post-traumatic stress-related symptoms

A person's capacity to grow in awareness, learning, and lifestyle changes will influence any selected treatment choices and success potential. As there are many individual differences and variations in the type and severity of bipolar conditions, the needs and type of treatment will vary or differ from person to person.

A BETTER TREATMENT MODEL FOR BPI

A broader, holistic healthcare model would have a better potential for improved research, diagnosis, and BPI treatment. An integrative model might include:

- Nutrition and dietary habits
- Genetics and family history
- Spirituality
- Social psychology and support systems
- Exercise physiology and skills
- Endocrinology and health of regulatory hormones
- Environmental medicine and allergies
- Mind/body/spiritual integration and well-being

People with bipolar illness are often misdiagnosed as having depression or other conditions, and then receive treatment that often results in a poor treatment outcome. These individuals would respond better to a broader, holistic and integrative type of treatment program, such as the one that had benefited Ben's recovery (as described above). Early recognition, comprehensive assessment, and an integrative approach to treatment, including natural therapies, can help bipolar sufferers improve their overall health, thereby improving their chances of stabilization, better relationships, productivity, and a stable work life. As proper assessment and diagnosis can be of critical importance, seeking a skilled, holistic and experienced healthcare practitioner is often essential, preferably a healthcare provider trained in mental health work.

TIPS: NATURAL NON-MEDICATION APPROACHES

Some non-medication or more natural approaches to treating BPI are:
- Improving lifestyle, nutrition, exercise, and sleep
- Addressing environmental issues
- Stress management or reduction
- Individual or group psychotherapy
- Avoidance of alcohol and substance abuse
- Educational, behavioral, family, cognitive, or trauma therapy
- Other complementary mind-body-spiritual oriented programs

Other complementary practices or therapies are:

- Relaxation training, yoga
- Oriental medicine, acupuncture
- Religious, meditation, and spiritual practices
- Regular exercise and sleep
- Using fish oil, rich in EPA and DHA, which can complement other BPI treatments

Nutrition and specific dietary programs are potentially helpful in the treatment of mood disorders. Diets reported as beneficial are those designed by a nutritionist, with needed levels of:

- Healthy fats
- Vegetables, rich in minerals and anti-oxidants
- Quality protein sources and foods
- Regulated sugar and starch content (low or avoided when over-weight, prediabetic, or diabetic)
- Gluten-free for those intolerant, reactive, or sensitive to gluten. (Gluten is found in wheat, rye, barley, and in processed foods and is considered a trigger in some people for inflammatory and autoimmune diseases).

If carefully used under the guidance of an experienced healthcare provider, specially designed, full-spectrum lights are sometimes useful (especially if there is a seasonal component to depression and mood cycling). Likewise, allergic or environmental problems benefit from assessing and correcting any nutritional, metabolic, and hormonal problems (such as thyroid deficiencies).

A biochemical, genetic problem, called hypomethylation, might improve with nutrition, and there is evidence that it affects the expression of bipolar symptoms. Methylation is also relevant to drug-nutrient interaction in BPI treatment and is one of the possible underlying factors contributing to medications not working effectively.

MEDICATION CONSIDERATIONS FOR PRACTITIONERS

For practitioners, some considerations for medication interventions and treatment are:

- Worsening of BPI with inadequate response to non-medication approaches
- Development of thought or cognitive impairment, such as psychotic symptoms with delusions, hallucinations, or dangerous behavior, especially when accompanied by poor judgment and risk of harm to self or other
- Actual or imminent need for a safe protective environment such as a psychiatric hospital or ward
- Lack of capacity or willingness to follow non-medication treatment regimens or protocols
- Patient's choice of medication treatment over non-medication (after being fully educated about all options, including therapy programs or natural alternatives, and about the risk of using medicines versus not taking them; the potential for adverse immediate or long-term risks; or side effects from medication)

According to some studies, those with bipolar disorder, if not treated with medication or a mood-stabilizing agent when needed, have a significant risk for more severe disease and chronic illness with frequent relapses. More than 50 percent of people will abuse drugs or alcohol, if BP illness goes unrecognized and untreated.

MEDICATION AND RISK

When considering prescribing a particular psychoactive medication, practitioners need to weigh several factors, such as:

1. **Potential for short-term or long-term side effects**, such as weight gain, diabetes, metabolic problems, high blood pressure, heart disease, abnormal restlessness, involuntary movement disorders of the face,

mouth, and limb (mostly a risk with antipsychotic medication and possibly from some antidepressants)

2. **Potential for making mood cycling worse** *or triggering episodes of mania or psychosis*

That said, there are several classes of medications to consider, including:

1. **Antidepressants,** such as selective serotonin reuptake inhibitors (SSRIs) that alter chemical nerve factors (neurotransmitters) to help depression

2. **Anxiolytics**, such as anxiety-reducing medication that supports the neurotransmitter GABA, which helps relieve anxiety

3. **Mood stabilizers,** such as those that help balance and stabilize brain activity and neurotransmitters (active brain chemicals), which can also have an anti-depressant and anti-anxiety effect

4. **Antipsychotic medication** can help eliminate or reduce psychotic thoughts (abnormal or disturbed thinking, such as delusions and hallucinations), reduce agitation, stabilize mood, and reduce depression

Weighing the potential risk of medications versus the benefits requires discussion. Any use of medicines should be a part of a well-designed comprehensive treatment program.

Appreciating the many facets of BPI, the varied presentation and potential for adverse impact on people's lives, underscores the importance of early recognition, assessment, and initiation of comprehensive and holistic/integrative treatment. Effective treatment of BPI sufferers can bring a more stable, functional, fulfilling, and productive life.[20]

DEPRESSION TREATMENT

Peter* hit bottom after working for two months as a nursing assistant on a hospital intensive care unit. He saw two or three deaths per day in patients with COVID-19 infections.

He became increasingly distraught after experiencing so many deaths and the grieving of loved ones. His distress grew with the pressure of non-stop work, frequent missed meals, and working additional shifts during a healthcare worker shortage. He was also under constant fear of catching the infection, mostly because of a lack of PPE and fresh N95 masks and plastic shields. Because of exposure and possibly carrying the disease, he also lived away from his family and girlfriend.

He became increasingly tired, with difficulty getting enough sleep, lacking energy, not feeling much motivation to do things, or enjoying much of anything at all, including eating the food he liked. His sleep involved frequent anxiety, dreams, and nightmares. He became jumpier, startled more easily, and began having recurrences of the panic attacks he had suffered after returning from being a medic during the Iraqi war. The VA had thought he had some PTSD and briefly treated him with a mild tranquilizer and antidepressants. He didn't like the meds, stopped after several weeks, and just pushed his way through, *busy with his life and a new job. He did no therapy work, as they had suggested.*

When very dark thoughts filled his mind, he became fearful of going crazy or getting sick and dying. He made some comments to fellow workers and one nurse on the unit where he worked. They were alarmed and insisted that he see someone at the employee health service and employee assistance program, who felt he needed a mental health evaluation. He went to his family doctor, who referred him to a psychiatrist. An antidepressant was prescribed, and he was referred to a therapist with experience working with depression and trauma.

Peter didn't begin the antidepressants right away because of the many concerns, including his prior poor tolerance, worry about side effects, and long-term consequences. His therapist made sure he got time off from work and began an integrative program with him. The program included trauma-focused therapy, addressing some underpinnings for his PTSD, including some earlier life trauma experience, overall poor health, lack of healthy exercise and diet, sedentary lifestyle outside of his work, and poor relationships with significant others. He also took time to discuss some of his issues around his reluctance to take medication.

Peter did eventually add the antidepressant medication to his program and tolerated it. In the following weeks, he gradually improved and returned to work, where there was a great need. He felt more secure in doing so, as he was on a better overall health program, was more fortified to cope with the stress, and knew how to reach out for help when he needed it.

(*To protect confidentiality, this story is a composite of some clinical experiences and does not represent an actual person or any prior patients).

STUDIES REVEAL SIDE EFFECTS OF ANTI-DEPRESSANTS

Most antidepressant prescriptions are written by non-psychiatric or mental health trained healthcare providers, who are often the initial access point for mental health care. Antidepressants are the third most frequently prescribed medications in the U.S. By some reports, about one tenth of this country's adults are taking antidepressants. However, studies and patient experiences reveal unwanted side effects.

Caution and careful assessment and monitoring remain vital in determining antidepressant safety and use for specific patients. Areas of concern are antidepressant use during pregnancy, in children or in adolescents, with the potential link between selective serotonin reuptake inhibitor (SSRI) use and suicide attempt or completion, and other possible adverse health outcomes.

The linking of antidepressants to severe adverse outcomes or side effects remains a concern and a cause for vigilance, caution, and the need for continued research. Reports of severe adverse consequences show varying levels of evidence to support the potential for danger; however, the typical side effects of medications do occur. Still, the ultimate proof that there is an actual link to an increase in autism, violence, or suicidality in younger age groups remains an ongoing area of investigation. Likewise, some studies have linked SSRI antidepressant usage during the second and third trimesters of the mother's pregnancy with autism spectrum disorders (ASD) in children.[21]

CONVENTIONAL DEPRESSION TREATMENT

Untreated depression can rob a person of their vitality, energy and motivation, and interfere with relationships, work, and life enjoyment. Depression can become chronic and grow into a more serious physical or mental illness, contributing to a loss of health; drug or alcohol abuse; and potential death by related medical illness, overdose, or suicide. **Therefore, there is a role for conventional treatments with medication, especially in resistant or major depression, where more natural therapies have not been effective.**

If other non-medication treatments are not available, when an adequate evaluation or consultation occurs by a qualified mental health practitioner, successful treatment with antidepressants—with or without a combination with more natural approaches–can be helpful and sometimes life-saving.

Antidepressants are a consideration when other non-medication therapies are unlikely to be beneficial, possible, or available. In such cases, there needs to be a clear clinical indication for the use of a medication or any proposed treatment.

DEPRESSION AND INTEGRATIVE PSYCHIATRY

From an integrative psychiatry perspective, before considering any medication, practitioners should consider *all* the dimensions that may affect a person and their illness. **Safe and more natural options are also crucial initial considerations.** Non-medication alternatives would depend on an individual's ability to learn and receive education about the steps in doing a therapeutic program, to comply with recommendations, and to have the support needed for the recommended plan.

The treated person would also need to have the willingness and resources to participate in any therapy recommended, whether natural approaches, psychotherapy, or medication combined with other modalities, or alone. The individual's medical or physical state, their potential for harm to self or others, or the risk of side effects from any treatment or medication use would need consideration. The risks versus benefits of any treatment would also require careful and critical review. Because of the concerns about potential side effects or long-term consequences of antidepressants, a thorough evaluation by a qualified medical and mental health practitioner with skills and expertise in working with mood difficulties is the best route.

BIPOLAR ILLNESS IN

STRESSFUL TIMES

At her family's insistence, Sarah* had several mental health evaluations. She had been married and divorced four times and was in and out of many jobs. She had an early life history of trauma, including at age 14 when her mother's live-in boyfriend sexually abused her. At age 15, further trauma occurred when Sarah was raped at a party. She occasionally had nightmares about the incidents and had flashbacks, or panic-like attacks, mostly when she smelled certain odors or sounds reminiscent of her rape. She had made several suicide attempts during recurring periods of severe depression, with two hospitalizations when her doctors considered her to be a danger to herself. Her mother and one aunt had a history of bipolar illness.

So far, Sarah had never experienced an intense period of mood activation or mania. However, one of her treating psychiatrists thought she had hypomania (milder periods of mood and behavior activation, or changes). A new diagnosis was given: Bipolar II type of BPI and post-traumatic stress disorder (PTSD). Sarah received appropriate treatment and sought a holistically oriented health care provider, who encouraged her to *follow a more optimal health, nutritional, and spiritual lifestyle program.* (*To protect confidentiality, the above is a composite of some clinical experiences and does not represent an actual person or any prior patients).

CHOOSING HEALTH

In this story, Sarah's family and significant others began to pay attention and take action when her milder, everyday life difficulties became more dramatic, extreme, and destructive. If you, a family member, or someone you know shows unusual shifts in mood and energy with uncharacteristic behaviors, it may be an early sign of bipolar illness (BPI).

In such cases, finding a trained professional is often necessary when mood changes are severe, persistent, and interfering with daily life. It is important to identify BPI early in its course and to get treatment through a comprehensive, holistic treatment program. If not, the illness can have devastating effects on relationships, careers, and health—as was Sarah's situation.

RECOGNIZING BPI IN ALL ITS FORMS

Recurrence of bipolar episodes with depression, anxiety, mania, or hypomania has adverse effects on family, social, and occupational functioning. BPI disrupts many typical day-to-day activities in areas as:

- Social functioning and relationships
- Work and productivity
- Sleep and physical health

The illness can also lead to flawed thinking (cognition), poor judgments, increased distractibility (poor focus), dysphoria (sad moods), and physical discomfort with increased preoccupations with health problems. There can be compromised functioning as with:

- More impulsive or volatile behaviors or self-expression
- Loss of interest, pleasure, and motivation in doing things
- Suicidal thinking

Other commonly associated symptoms may include:

- Inflated self-esteem or grandiosity
- Decreased need to sleep
- Being more talkative than usual, or a pressure to keep talking
- Flight of ideas, or the experience of racing thoughts
- Distractibility
- Increase goal-directed activity
- Excessive involvement in high-risk activities
- Marked impairment in social and work functioning
- Sometimes a need for hospitalization (if the potential for harm to self or others, poor judgment, or thought disturbance, such as psychotic symptoms)

BPI's early appearance is often not recognized by significant others or by healthcare providers. A key feature that separates the illness from recurring depression is the occurrence of hypomania or a more severe manic episode. A manic episode is a period of elevated, expansive, or irritable moods, and increases goal-directed activity or energy, often lasting for at least a week.

In Bipolar I disorder, the manic episode may have been preceded or followed by hypomania or major depressive episodes. Bipolar II disorder, by definition, includes no manic episode. Some subtler conditions can present with milder and more difficult-to-recognize symptoms, such as irritability, anxiety, and moodiness, alternating with less pronounced depression periods. For the entire BPI range in its varying expression, another classification is bipolar spectrum illness: this would include even the less recognizable forms of recurrent depression with milder periods of activation, hypomania, and less dramatic symptoms.

For more information on BPI, go to the American Psychiatric Association (APA) website for their current definition. This official nomenclature has also been codified and defined in the *DSM-5* (a manual published by the APA).[22]

CAN DEPRESSION BE BIPOLAR ILLNESS?

Recurrent depression is often bipolar illness unrecognized. Additional clues to underlying BPI include:

- Inadequate response to treatment for depression
- Manic or psychotic symptoms
- Manic mood fluctuations triggered by antidepressants
- Family history of bipolar illness
- Onset or recurrent depression before 20 years of age
- Severe premenstrual syndrome, PMS, or premenstrual dysphoria syndrome (PMDS)
- Postpartum depression
- Atypical depression with a lot of irritability, sleep disturbance, and anxiety

At its worst, BPI can lead to higher mortality from suicide and other co-occurring medical illnesses. Among psychiatric disorders, BPI has a significant risk of death from suicide. According to some studies, the risk in BP II types of BPI for suicide is more significant than in BP I. When BPI occurs with other mental or physical illnesses that go unrecognized, it can lead to ineffective treatment and poor outcomes. For example, six months after suffering a myocardial infarction, victims with major depression—commonly seen in BPI—had six times the mortality rate of non-depressed patients. Presentation of BPI in the older population (that is, older than 50 years) will often have other medical problems at the time of diagnosis, including cognitive changes. More than 50 percent will abuse drugs or alcohol if BPI is not recognized and treated.

MILD BPI CAN ALSO MIMIC STRESS

Bipolar illness is frequently unrecognized, resulting in unnecessary distress and suffering. People with this disorder are sometimes misdiagnosed as having only depression and then treated, often resulting in a poor treatment outcome. Such individuals might respond better to a bipolar-illness-focused treatment program. **A holistic or integrative approach to the study and treatment of BPI offers a better path to understanding, treatment, and prevention of future illness.**[23] With a broader integrative healthcare model, there is the potential for improved research, diagnosis, and BPI treatment. Effective outcomes can happen with patience and commitment to finding an appropriate care and treatment program, as occurred with Sarah.

HOLISTIC APPROACHES TO
POST-TRAUMATIC STRESS

Martha* was a well-liked and excellent eighth-grade teacher in her inner-city school. Her students admired her understanding, effective teaching, and leadership in several extracurricular programs. One day, she came to work visibly shaken, reporting that two older teens had pushed her down and stolen her purse. Two weeks after this occurrence, arriving at school a half-hour early to catch up on some paperwork, a large man suddenly shoved her through the entrance door. She screamed but stopped when hit with a weapon by the attacker. Some other staff and students arrived, causing the nervous assailant to turn and flee. Martha then went to her physician, and after a few days, she felt well enough to return to work.

Over the next few weeks, Marth felt easily distracted and startled, especially by sudden movement or noise. Her sleep became disrupted by nightmares of being attacked or chased. For the first time, she began having what she and others described as panic attacks: with the sudden onset of a rapid pounding heart, an overwhelming feeling of dread that something terrible would happen, and an urge to flee or leave the room. She could no longer drive, as panic attacks would occur when traveling in a car. She had to take sick leave from her teaching work, and she sought professional help.

The first doctor felt she had attention deficit hyperactivity disorder (ADHD), yet the medication prescribed only made her worse. She went to someone else, who felt that her primary problem was depression and anxiety. He tried prescribing an antidepressant, which did not work, and he then wanted to change her to a bipolar condition medication. At that point, she sought a different health care provider.

A therapist was recommended, someone specialized and experienced with specific, trauma-related therapy and treatment. Martha also saw a holistic physician who helped her improve her lifestyle, nutrition, and exercise program. Martha reported she had experienced sexual and verbal abuse as a child, growing up with an alcoholic mother and an often-absent father during that time. Her peers had often bullied her as a shy child. Martha's recovery was gradual, but she ultimately resumed her classroom work with her students after three or four months.

(*To protect the confidentiality, the above is a composite of some clinical experiences and does not represent an actual person or any prior patients).

TRAUMA IN THE GENERAL POPULATION

As we've discussed, trauma and trauma-related mental health conditions is an essential topic of the day, with mental health practitioners seeing a marked rise in people asking for help during the COVID-19 pandemic. There has been an unprecedented number of deaths and severe COVID-19 related illnesses, and front-line medical workers have experienced overwhelming demands and losses from the disease's ravages—comparable to medical doctors and soldiers in a war zone.

It is valuable to focus on what we know about trauma and the development of trauma-related illnesses to guide our work on prevention, early recognition, treatment, and recovery. About eight million adults have PTSD during any year, representing only a small portion of those who have ever experienced trauma. About 70 percent of adults in the U.S. have experienced a traumatic event at least once in their lifetime. Ten percent or more of these people will develop PTSD, according to some studies. One out of nine women will develop PTSD, or about twice the rate for men.

Current statistics on post-traumatic stress disorder (PTSD) and trauma-related disorders (or TRI, also referred to as trauma spectrum disorders) show a significantly increased occurrence. Factors responsible for the rise in PTSD include environmental catastrophes such as wildfires, droughts, hurricanes, and flooding; infectious pandemics; war; and the growing violence in our society. As a result, mental health practitioners are seeing more victims and sufferers from the effects of trauma. Most people would not expect trauma-related illnesses and PTSD to show up from events outside of war, the military, and severe accidents, and so people affected often go unrecognized and never seek treatment. They continue to suffer the ill effects of trauma and its aftermath.

The effects of trauma and its aftermath can occur to anyone at any life stage from childhood through adulthood. The trauma itself can result from a wide variety of experiences:

- Exposure to threatened death, serious injury, auto accidents, or violence
- Feeling helpless during trauma such as childhood sexual abuse, rape, physical assaults
- Significant, overwhelming, adverse, and life-threatening events (earlier in life or in adulthood) or poly-trauma (i.e., series of traumatic events: as a job loss, divorce, death of a significant other)
- Sudden or significant emotional losses
- Witnessing domestic violence, death, or injury to others
- Natural disasters or mass causality events, such as a terrorist attack

Also, many contributing factors can make an individual more vulnerable to PTSD or TRI, including earlier life traumas as listed above, and some of the following additional vulnerability factors:

- Minimal social support
- History of another physical or mental health problem, or substance use disorder
- Recent losses
- Contributing genetic factors

The annual cost to our medical care system is immense for PTSD, TRI, and improper treatment. Beyond the actual treatment, the costs include expenses from unemployment, drug use, other associated illnesses, disabilities, and death.

For a detailed description of trauma-related illness and PTSD symptoms, see the American Psychiatric Association's official *Diagnostic and Statistical Manual of Mental Disorders, 5th Edition (DSM-5).*[24] Intermittent or chronic emotional or physical symptoms that may be a sign of TRI or PTSD from prior trauma or trauma exposure include:

1. **Reliving:** People with PTSD repeatedly relive the ordeal through thoughts and intrusive memories of the trauma, including flashbacks, hallucinations, nightmares, feeling great distress when reminded of the trauma, or acting and feeling as if the trauma were recurring and psychologically distressing.

2. **Avoiding or feeling numb:** The person may avoid people, places, thoughts, or situations that remind him or her of the trauma; have an inability to recall an aspect of the trauma; feel detached or estranged from others; isolate and withdraw from family and friends; lose interest in activities that the person once enjoyed; have difficulty experiencing love, joy or intimacy; sense a restricted range of feelings; develop difficulty relating to others; report diminished interest or participation in significant activities; and experience a sense of a foreshortened future.

3. **Increased emotional arousal:** excessive worry or guilt; difficulty falling or staying asleep; feeling nervous or fearful; increased

irritability; outbursts of anger and agitation; difficulty concentrating; hyper-vigilance, guardedness, or increased alertness; physiological reactivity upon exposure to trauma cues; and having exaggerated startle responses or being jumpy.

4. Experiencing **worsening physical symptoms and medical problems**: e.g., increased blood pressure and heart rate, fatigue, rapid breathing, muscle tension, headaches, sweating, digestive problems, poor appetite, nausea, and diarrhea.

The onset of trauma-related symptoms or illness sometimes happens months after the traumatizing event. However, these and other symptoms may appear earlier. Intervention with therapies now available can help bring relief.

INTEGRATIVE TREATMENT

An integrated, holistic approach brings together the tools, practices, and scope of integrative psychiatry, psychology, and medicine. The goal would be early recognition, assessment, diagnosis, and treatment of people with symptoms or problems resulting from trauma. First in the treatment process would be an investigation into contributing factors related to prior traumatic exposures. The practitioner would look for: environmental, genetics, medical, psychological, developmental, and/or family history issues. The tools of integrated psychiatry and psychology would include in-depth clinical history and psycho-social assessment, physical examination, psychological testing, consulting with significant other (such as family members), laboratory testing, and finally, developing a comprehensive treatment program.

The holistic and integrative health care practitioner's role would be to add their unique skills and knowledge to the treatment and management of any individuals with TRI or PTSD. As there is often dysfunction or problems in multiple areas, a careful diagnostic evaluation needs to occur. Any corrective interventions will then help to ease symptoms or illnesses. Intervention may include treatment for such conditions as infections, digestive disturbance, nutritional or hormonal imbalances, allergies, drug or alcohol addiction, emotional and mood issues, and personal or family stressors. Treatment can improve comfort, well-being, sleep, and restoration as well as enhance autonomic regulation.

Treatment options would include:

- Lifestyle and nutritional improvements
- Reduction in psycho-social stressors
- Individual or group psychotherapies, especially trauma-focused therapies, that address current or past developmental and trauma issues
- Interventions as suggested by clinical findings and lab tests

When non-medication interventions, including the search for other contributing factors, are not helpful, the next step may be medication. Medications commonly considered are:

- Selective serotonin reuptake inhibitors for depression and anxiety (SSRIs, e.g., fluoxetine, sertraline)
- Symptomatic treatments with sleep agents such as prazosin, an anti-hypertensive medication that is helpful for PTSD nightmares in adults
- Benzodiazepines (tranquilizers), although long-term use does not appear beneficial, and it is challenging to wean and stop
- β-blockers, which are used to reduce arousal but are otherwise of questionable benefit

If there has been significant trauma and apparent TRI or PTSD, a team or network approach would be optimal; this would include health care practitioners trained in the modalities referred to above, plus the presence of and needed interventions by an experienced trauma therapist. Therapy may involve different approaches depending on the training of the trauma therapist, such as:

- Individual or group psychotherapy
- Behavioral or cognitive-behavioral therapy (CBT)

- Exposure therapy, trauma-focused cognitive-behavioral therapy, trauma systems therapy
- Body-mind therapies, somatic experiencing, eye movement desensitization and reprocessing (EMDR), Emotional Freedom Technique, Reset therapy[25]
- Other natural alternatives or medication

When indicated, procedures or lab testing can help determine difficulties with conditions such as nutrition and digestion, thyroid and hormones, blood chemistry, complete blood count, abnormal blood sugar, lipids, B-12, folic acid levels, and vitamin D 25-hydroxy levels. (More specific and advanced testing can also be ordered, if indicated.) Such treatment helps reduce stress from contributing psychosocial and medical factors, promotes restorative sleep, and reduces pain and discomfort. Relief from environmental-related illness, allergies, and traumatic memories are possible added benefits, which allow more opportunity for the body, mind, and spirit to recover from trauma wounds.

TIPS: ADDRESSING TRAUMA

Be knowledgeable and prepared. Know the signs of trauma. If you or anyone you know exhibits TRI symptoms or PTSD, they need your support, help, or encouragement. Healing or reducing somatic, emotional, mental, and spiritual issues and other factors contributing to the severity of TRI and PTSD—in conjunction with medication when needed—has the potential for relief and the reduction of suffering from illness associated with recent or prior trauma.[26]

ADDICTIONS UNCOVERED

It was a damp and cold day with a slight overcast that fit the funeral's somber mood. My father had died, leaving many stories untold. I was the youngest son, to whom he had often confided, and I often thought he might not have revealed to my brothers the personal stuff he shared with me.

After my father's solemn burial at the cemetery, his younger brother, my uncle, took my hand. I gladly followed him away from my father's burial site and the family members there. We reached the furthest and less-visited part of the cemetery, filled with older gravestones. My uncle pointed to a headstone with hard-to-read engravings that had tilted to the left, sunk partway into the ground.

He said, "This is the tombstone of my father, your grandfather; he was a drunk with the worst alcoholism imaginable. Your grandmother took over the family grocery store business and divorced our father after he disappeared for some years. She had to save all of us kids from being out on the streets. Our father continued, apparently, to drink after he left. When he reappeared, he was in a very degenerated condition and, after medical care, ended up in a nursing home until he died."

My father's sister, my aunt, had a much more romantic tale. Her story about my grandfather was of his migration from a European country with the challenge of fitting into U.S. society—a situation made worse by his poor command of the *language. He found some comrades in a local community religious group and would often stay out late with them, sometimes at the expense of his struggling family. Even though he was a well-educated man in his country of origin, life was hard for him, and he didn't adapt very well. Also, he reportedly had great disappointment when his sister, to whom he had been very close, left their home and married a man of another background and religion, which was not accepted by the family. My aunt reported that my grandfather became very discouraged and depressed and never recovered.*

I then remembered, a little while after, that my father had told me some tidbits about my grandfather. My father said that his father was irresponsible with their family, staying out late drinking with his friends. It was a painful experience growing up in their early years with an unavailable and neglectful parent who eventually deserted them.

UNRECOGNIZED ADDICTION

This personal remembrance reflects how addiction's tragedy affects so many families, each with their own stories to tell. Current statistics show the immensity and seriousness of unrecognized substance abuse disorders and addictions. **An integrative psychiatry perspective looks beyond labels, symptoms, or a few characteristics to find understanding and positive treatment options for substance use problems.**

HOW SERIOUS IS THE PROBLEM?

Since 2000, over 700,000 drug overdose deaths have occurred in the U.S. The federal budget for drug control in 2020 was $34.6 billion. The total economic cost of addictions, alcoholism, and drug abuse would be much higher when including:

- The expense of treatment and preventive programs
- Additional related health care costs
- Reduced job productivity and loss of earnings

- Increased crime with resulting personal and public costs
- Social welfare needs

In 2017, 67.8% of the 70,237 drug overdose deaths were opioid-related (heroin, fentanyl morphine, and other prescription opioid pain relievers). 19.4% of people in the U.S. used illicit drugs in 2018. Also in 2018, 20.3 million people in the U.S. aged 12 or older had a substance abuse disorder, 14.8 million with alcohol and 8.1 million with illegal drugs—with the most common being marijuana, and 2 million with an opioid disorder (including prescription pain reliever and heroin abuse). In the same year, accidental drug overdose was the leading cause of death among persons less than 45 years old.[27]

LEGAL SUBSTANCES ARE PART OF THE PICTURE

In the recent past, healthcare practitioners learned to treat pain with drugs, which are now known to cause addiction. Patients taking the pills trusted the prevailing belief that there would be pain control with a low risk of addiction. Since then, prescriptions for pain medicine, such as opiates, have soared. Unfortunately, people prescribed opioids for pain can develop opioid use disorders and be at risk of dying from an overdose. Opioid overdose deaths since have multiplied, and yet opioid prescriptions have increased markedly. Today, many who received long-term opioid therapy in primary care settings struggle with opioid addiction.

IS SUGAR ADDICTIVE?

Overuse of refined carbohydrates, aka sugar, is considered a contributor to obesity, diabetes, heart disease, and other health issues; thus, it resembles the abuse or addiction to other substances. Though an addiction-like problem, it is often overlooked, especially with the massive marketing of sweetened products and their ready availability at many food outlets and restaurants. Some characteristics of sugar addiction even resemble the symptoms of cocaine addiction.[28]

ADDICTION DEFINED

The American Society of Addiction Medicine (ASAM, 2020) defines addiction as a "treatable, chronic medical disease involving complex interactions among brain circuits, genetics, the environment, and an individual's life experiences. People with addiction use substances or engage in behaviors that become compulsive and often continue despite harmful consequences." Addictions present characteristically in several ways:[29]

- Pathologically pursuing reward and relief by substance use and other behaviors
- Inability to consistently abstain
- Impairment in behavioral control
- Craving
- Diminished recognition of significant problems with one's actions and interpersonal relationships
- Dysfunctional emotional response
- Cycles of relapse and remission

The *Diagnostic and Statistical Manual of Mental Disorders (5th Edition) (DSM-5)* from the American Psychiatric Association replaced the term "addiction" with "substance use disorder." The replacement occurred because the term "addiction" had an uncertain definition and possible negative connotations. "Substance use disorder" became a more neutral term and implies a more extensive range of dysfunction, from mild to the severe state of "chronic relapsing and compulsive drug-taking and alcohol use." However, the word "addiction" is still commonly used in the U.S. and other countries:

- It applies if there is the persistence of severe substance abuse problems, as when there are at least two significant occurrences within 12 months
- The substance is used in larger amounts or over a more extended period than intended
- There is a persistent desire or unsuccessful effort to cut down or control the substance use

- Spending more time in activities necessary to get the substance, to use a drug, or to recover from its effects
- Craving or a strong desire to use the substance
- Continued use, despite persistent or recurrent social or interpersonal problems that are caused or exacerbated by effects of the substance
- Important social, occupational, or recreational activities are stopped or reduced because of the substance use
- Recurrent substance use occurs in situations in which it is physically hazardous
- Continued use of the substance, despite knowledge of having a persistent or current physical or psychological problem that is likely caused or exacerbated by the substance
- Tolerance is a need for markedly increased amounts of the substance to achieve the desired effect
- Withdrawal shows the characteristics of withdrawal syndrome for the particular substance
- Related substances are used to relieve or to avoid withdrawal symptoms

The *DSM-5* similarly describes alcohol and opioids, as both are considered "use disorders with problematic patterns of use, leading to clinically significant impairment or distress."[30]

RISK FACTORS

Many factors can increase the risk of developing an addiction. A family history of addiction can increase the likelihood of substance use disorders in relatives. One national co-morbidity survey showed that individuals with a mood disorder are 2.3 times more likely to have a substance use disorder than those without a mood disorder. For bipolar disorder, there is a 9.7 times greater chance of having alcohol dependence and an 8.4 times higher chance of having another type of drug dependence. Trauma-related conditions, such as the experience of a traumatic childhood or adult life events, are common underpinnings of addiction. Attention deficit hyperactivity disorder (ADHD), anxiety, obsessive-compulsive disorder, and schizophrenic disorders have higher associated substance abuse rates. Given these statistics, recognition and treatment of any condition that can potentiate or put one at risk for addiction need attention as soon as possible.

EARLY WARNING SIGNS

The early warning signs of drug and alcohol abuse include:

- Increased drinking or use of other drugs
- Changes in a job or school performance
- Changes in attitude and mood, such as depression, irritability, suicidal threats, or actions
- Unexplained changes in eating, sleeping habits, physical appearance, physical complaints, blackouts, or temporary memory loss
- Behavioral problems such as dishonesty, sexual promiscuity, and stealing
- Change in relationships, especially with new friends known to drink or use drugs
- Alcohol on one's breath, slurred speech, staggering, appearing "spaced out"
- Missing alcohol, medications, or money from around the house
- The presence of drug paraphernalia, such as pipes, pillboxes, etc.

Noticing these signs is critical, as recognition, early interventions, and treatment are vital to improved health. The goal of any treatment would be to reduce pain and suffering as well as the staggering cost to society. Because addictions can switch, symptoms need early recognition and intervention. Examples would be shifting between compulsive eating, gambling, the internet, computer use, and sexual or pornography addictions. There are valuable screening tools and questionnaires available to identify many addictions. The AUDIT for alcohol and the SBIRT for alcohol and substance abuse are helpful.

NEW RESEARCH ON BRAIN FUNCTION

It is also useful to learn how the brain develops, perpetuates addictions, and can heal itself. Robust mechanisms in our nervous systems and brain serve positive purposes. These critical brain operations are for survival, food, shelter, reward, gratification, and reproduction. The same processes are also the miraculous pathway for the achievement of success and accomplishments. Misdirection can occur, however, diverging into debilitating addiction and substance use disorders.[31]

As we've seen, the brain can adapt, change, and lay down new neurocircuitry (nerve pathways). "Neuroplasticity" is the descriptive name for this ability of the brain to change. Less-used neurocircuitry will wither away in a healing and regenerative process. Information is growing about the brain's operations, functioning, and influencers. And the application of gained knowledge in neurological research can lead to positive treatment outcomes, with goals of prevention, restoration of health, and addiction recovery.

The neuroplasticity process underpins the changes that can occur with training and positive addiction treatment programs. Changes in neurotransmitter patterns can cause new positive habits and behaviors. Training and positive experience in supportive social settings support these brain changes.[32]

INTEGRATIVE MEDICINE FOR ADDICTION

Integrative and comprehensive approaches to addiction treatment are essential. Other techniques, such as trauma-oriented therapies as EMDR and Spiritual Emergence, are potentially valuable additions to treatment programs. The Spiritual Emergence approach, as an example, aims to help people live to their fullest potential. A transpersonal, systems-oriented, body-centered, and trauma-integrated process fosters healing and spiritual emergence from spiritual emergencies, mental health issues, and substance use disorders. Addressing the physical, emotional, mental, social, and spiritual aspects becomes the pathway to wholeness and wellness.[33]

A thorough addiction treatment approach looks at factors such as the environment, child-to-adulthood influences, psychosocial factors, trauma, and medical and neurodevelopmental issues. The importance of how other factors affect brain processes and human behavior needs continuing investigation.

An intervention or treatment program often depends on a qualified individual to do an addiction assessment. Adding an integrative psychiatrist and an addiction specialist to the treatment team can bring full focus to co-existing problems. Co-existing medical or other issues may need attention before addiction treatment can be successful or sustained.

Integrative psychiatry and addiction programs may include:

- Education
- Counseling
- Psychotherapy
- Inpatient rehabilitation
- Outpatient programs
- Partial hospitalization
- Halfway houses
- Cognitive-behavioral therapy
- Motivational interviewing
- 12-step programs
- Mutual help/support groups
- Mind-body-spiritual and sensory-based therapies
- Natural complementary therapies

Medication augmentation helps, especially when other interventions are unsuccessful. Drugs that help reduce cravings and relapses are most effective for opioids and tobacco. The medications available are only moderately effective for alcohol and minimally useful for stimulants, cannabis, inhalants, and other substances.

TIPS: FOR FAMILY, FRIENDS, AND CO-WORKERS

With the dramatic rise in death from heroin overdoses and the devastating effects of drugs and alcohol on individuals, families, and children, addiction is a problem that always needs attention. **If you, or a significant other, such as a spouse, friend, or employer, see early signs of addiction, do not ignore them, as you may inadvertently contribute to the problem's severity.** Instead, seek immediate help and information for both the recognition and treatment of substance abuse to prevent serious consequences.

Seek or consult with:

- Health care providers or your primary care physician
- Addiction specialists, treatment centers, or programs
- Integrative psychiatrists or holistic health practitioners
- Twelve-step programs, such as Alcoholics Anonymous or Narcotics Anonymous
- Other recommended resources in this book's footnotes[34]

You can also find local resources in your community or on government or other reputable websites.

THE HEART-ADDICTION
CONNECTION

"This heart will one day find you a sweetheart. This soul will one day take you to the beloved. Seize your pain as a blessing. Your pain will one day lead you to heal."

- Rumi

I met "Buddy" when I was working in a West Coast emergency room. He came into the ER, looking pale and barely breathing. His overdose was thought at first to be from IV heroin, but it was because of Fentanyl: a synthetic form of a heroin-like opioid that is much more potent than heroin and more likely to cause overdose deaths. The EMT revived him with Narcan (a drug used in opioid overdoses).

Buddy received treatment just in time and avoided death. It was the second time in two months that this had occurred. Buddy did not seem any wiser after the nearly tragic outcome. Later I found out, to my dismay, that Buddy had been in a 28-day residential drug treatment program just before his recent overdose and near-death episode. He went to a drug detoxification facility after the ER and then to another 28-day residential drug rehabilitation program.

A year later, I again saw Buddy in the LA area. After another relapse with IV heroin, he entered a medication-assisted treatment program (MAT). The oral medication controlled his craving, the desire to reuse, and buy street drugs. He was also going several times per week to a Narcotics Anonymous twelve-step program. Drug addiction counseling and therapy continued through a community mental health service.

Ten years later, I again saw Buddy. This time, the circumstances had changed, and he was working as a licensed substance abuse counselor. He had ten-plus years of sobriety from the drug use that had almost cost him his life. The compassion in the community had helped, as he had the good fortune to access effective programs. He had become a student and practitioner of the art of being more present and in-the-moment. He was carrying a copy of Kornfield's book entitled No Time Like the Present.

Buddy had again found his passion, love, and connectedness with life. He felt an existence beyond his limited self-perception, constraining stories, and beliefs. Buddy was experiencing himself as a whole person, interconnected with his community and spirit. His healing was now a lifelong journey with recovery and helping others. There was a sense of liberation from his prison of avoidance, fear, and anger. He had grown into a spiritual warrior.

(*Buddy is a composite of patients treated for addiction and not an actual person.)

HARD TO IGNORE

A growing number of severe outcomes and deaths have occurred during the current opioid crisis, especially heroin and Fentanyl abuse. Substance use disorder and addictive illness now need bolder and more innovative programs. Awareness training and addiction education should be a part of every school curriculum. Selling and promoting drugs is a thriving industry in our country, without sufficient regulation or restraints to prevent negative impacts.

According to a recent government survey, the numbers are staggering:[35]

- 7.6% (18.7 MILLION) people aged 18 or older had a substance use disorder
- 11.4 million Americans misused opioids in 2017
- 2.1 million Americans have a diagnosed Opioid Use Disorder
- More than 70,000 drug overdose deaths in 2017—2/3 were related to heroin and synthetic opioids (e.g., Fentanyl)
- Heroin and illicit opioid pills contaminated by Fentanyl and other potent opioids are responsible for most deaths
- 45% of those affected by substance abuse had no treatment for heroin use disorder, and 79% had no treatment for prescription pain-reliever use disorder

Reasons cited for the lack of progress include:

- The stigma that keeps people away from needed treatment
- People's entrapment in views, opinions, and beliefs about addictive illness
- Inadequate addiction-focused education, resources, and providers
- Lack of integrative and holistic oriented programs, treatment availability, and community recovery supports
- Insufficiency of compassion and acceptance by significant others

TIPS: ADDICTION VULNERABILITY FACTORS

Determining your own or a loved one's level of risk to addiction can help detect early warning signs. A greater vulnerability may exist for addiction from early life trauma. Traumatic childhood experiences often occur during critical developmental years. It may arise from losses; abandonment; betrayals; neglect; and physical, emotional, and sexual abuse. All these can lead to the development of:

- Behavioral patterns and maladaptive defenses
- The feelings of insufficiency, lack, or low self-esteem
- Hypervigilance, panic, or anxiety
- Rage, anger, depression, or post-traumatic stress disorder (PTSD)

THE CORE OF SUBSTANCE ABUSE

Symbolically and poetically, the heart represents the natural emotional experience like love, passion, and connection. In ancient times, the heart was the connection to the divine and to the soul.

As a physical organ, the heart is in the center of the body. The pump circulates blood, nourishment, regulatory hormones, vitality, and warmth to the body; the heart becomes a representative of emotional states like compassion, passion, and love. The heart expression may also represent the holistic union of mind, body, feelings, love, emotions, and spirit. In ancient Pali and Sanskrit Buddhist scriptures, words such as "citta" represented "heart-mind." One would be in a state of unity in the consciousness of both thoughts and emotions. With meditation and mindfulness practices, the "mindfulness of mind" happens. An enlightened and liberated mind would provide the ground for the union of thoughts, emotions, and spiritual essence.[36]

In the world of addictions, there is often an avoidance or numbing towards feelings—especially anger, fear, aversion, and hatred. Avoidance can lead to rigid adherence to limiting behaviors, thoughts, opinions, and beliefs. A desperate search for relief, gratification, and sources of pleasure can ensue. Vulnerabilities can then develop to substances or drugs to help avoid pain, discomfort, and suffering.

We need to uncover a deeper understanding of addiction—get to the "heart of the matter." The hope would be to reorient our thinking to develop better approaches and treatment.[37] Losing a connection with the heart has meaning beyond the real, physical heart. The balance of mind, body, emotions, and spiritual attunement is vital for mental health and well-being.

PART III: COPING WITH TRAUMATIC EVENTS

MOURNING PET LOSS

I was working at my desk in my dream, and I saw my little Yorkie, Pepper, rolling and frolicking on the couch on his blanket. I got up to rub his tummy, which he always loved when he was on his back. As I approached him, I said, "You have died and will disappear when I get close." To my surprise, he stayed on his back and let us both enjoy and relish my rubbing of his belly. I woke up realizing that my hands were rubbing my own head and hair.

A CHANCE MEETING

A coincidence occurred, which seemed meant to be—a destiny or kismet, which was logically unexplainable. Carl Jung, the famous psychiatrist, called a meaningful chance happening "synchronicity." While my wife and I were in a food store, we noticed a little pet adoption sign that led to a new puppy for us.

He was an adopted pet from an animal rescue program. The woman in charge of the dog rescue that day said, "We rarely get small dogs, especially Yorkies, but they gave one up for adoption and are coming in later this afternoon." After considering the options, we went back that afternoon. And there the little critter stood, with his restless energy, waiting for love. I need not say more. That new puppy, Pepper, who became our wonderful pet and companion for over 12 years, died recently of a combination of old age and ill-health. Pepper became pet number five for us: one of our favorites, and one of our most painful losses.

Grief and bereavement can become prolonged—reaching a level of severity, and suffering—with a significant impact on health and the ability to function and self-manage. Early in my psychiatry practice, I remember seeing someone over a two-year period who had prolonged severe depression and grief after losing two longtime pets. When this occurs, major depression or depression related to post-traumatic stress disorder (PTSD) would be a possibility.

An evaluation by a mental health professional would then be an appropriate step. There could be a range of recommendations after evaluation, including therapy, lifestyle interventions, medications, support groups, and the encouragement to reach out to others. The advice to get another pet is not always the best solution, or even possible, and special care is appropriate if there are complications of the grieving process.

MOURNING VARIES ACCORDING TO SEVERAL FACTORS

The length and quality of the relationship with the pet, and the attachment that results, are significant. There often is more attachment when the pet has been an intimate or emotional support companion for many years. Some pets have been service, working, or therapy animals. After losing a pet, pain and suffering can be just as severe as losing a person, whether the pet owner has only one or multiple pets.

There may also be a history of multiple losses or traumas related to significant others' deaths in the past. A accumulative effect of partially-worked-through grief can result from an incomplete healing process of prior losses. If so, a person can be very vulnerable to another unexpected loss when past pain and trauma remain unprocessed, a vulnerability that affects adjustment to future adverse life situations and relationships. And the impact of COVID-19, which has heightened many people's feelings of insecurity, is undoubtedly a type of risk factor. In any of these instances, an individual with little "grieving reserve" or resilience may not move through a new grieving process healthily and adaptively.

DEALING WITH A LOSS

It is sometimes a matter of survival for an individual—who experiences an overwhelming trauma or shock—to go into denial of what has happened, especially if there is not much reserve or experience dealing with loss. In those cases, working through loss or trauma is often delayed for a later time when other factors and support might be more favorable. A more suitable time can then occur for experiencing and dissipating the pent-up feeling and emotion. Until then, what has accumulated under the surface of awareness, repressed or suppressed by the mind, can be comparable to a pressure cooker that always needs careful attendance and vigilance, so it won't explode. Waiting for a safer, less stressful time to process and work through a traumatic loss is often essential, so more attention can be placed on basic survival needs, especially when proper support or helpful resources for grief work are not available.

In Elisabeth Kübler-Ross's book *On Death and Dying*, five stages of grief and loss are related to losing any loved one or significant other.[38] Our previous chapter on "Depression and Grief" discusses the painful situation of losing a spouse with subsequent prolonged grief and depression. Some aspects of each Kübler-Ross stage of grief and loss can frequently happen after losing a pet. So it is worth rethinking these stages as they apply after losing a loved pet and companion.

1. **Denial stage**: Denial can happen after a loss with intense feelings like shock, disbelief, confusion, fear, avoidance, and emotional numbing. Agitation may occur being "hyper" and highly anxious; or possibly an inflated feeling of relief, of being a survivor when others have died.

2. **Anger stage:** The anger stage starts as the reality of the loss sets in. There can be emotions like feelings of blame towards oneself or others,

irritation, frustration, or nervousness. Anger may appear regarding the unfairness of life: "Why did this have to happen to my companion and me?"

3. **Bargaining stage:** Bargaining begins when the grieving person wonders whether there may have been actions that could have prevented the death, asking, "What if I had taken more appropriate measures or done things better or differently?" It is the time to reach out to others, to tell about or reflect on the loss, painful happening, and remembrances, with the struggle to find meaning in all of it.

4. **Depression stage:** This stage can be a challenge to experience or endure, especially when it shows up frequently or for prolonged periods. Depression can show up as:

   ◉ Sadness and grief

   ◉ Feeling helpless and hopeless

   ◉ Changes in appetite and sleep patterns

   ◉ Loss of one's usual vitality or interest in things

   ◉ Withdrawal and isolating self from others

   ◉ Not wanting to get out of bed

   ◉ Thoughts of self-harm or suicide

   ◉ **If a person feels that life has lost its meaning and is not worth living, or has suicidal thoughts, it is time to seek help from a mental healthcare provider.**

5. **Acceptance stage:** The residual feeling of loss, sadness, and grief with the reality of death's finality comes into a balance with acceptance, as the individual recognizes that life continues.

Many things can trigger a memory of the deceased: a picture, toys, grooming aids, or a time when doing a routine with a pet. For example, I just took a break from my writing and remembered that it would be the usual time to call my dog Pepper for a walk. Sometimes a dream will touch on some aspect of the grieving process. That opportunity provides for further reflection and working through the loss, grief, and painful emotions.

Sometimes there is the loss of a relationship that has been full of limitations on one's freedom, as seen in the long-term care of an ill or very dependent companion. Sometimes a person's life has acquired definition or meaning from their interactions, even within a very negative relationship. An example would be a pet that has reached a point of needing almost constant care or having a pet who is very destructive to property—your own and that of others—or sometimes being aggressive, biting, and/or becoming dangerous to others.

FACTORS THAT COMPLICATE THE RESOLUTION OF GRIEF

During a grief process, poor health or other risk factors can put a person at greater vulnerability. A survivor of a pet loss may have a higher risk of illness, or even death in the months following a traumatic loss (much as any older adult with impaired health). Lack of adequate support or care—including poor health and physical impairment—high-stress overload, mental or emotional illness (depression, PTSD), a history of multiple losses, trauma, or unresolved grief can all complicate the process.

Children who grow up on farms and who see farm animals' life and death are possibly better equipped to experience dying and others' deaths because of their early life exposure and learning. Conversely, survivors of war, severe accidents, trauma, or mass causality situations may have more difficulty or less resilience with any new trauma or loss, as seen in people living with PTSD.

SPIRITUAL ASPECTS OF LOSS

Having or losing a pet is an opening to the wisdom of loving, acceptance, letting go, embracing the totality of life, and of thinking beyond our own universe and small world, our limiting beliefs and perceptions. Grief or memories of lost companions or significant others never end, but they do change; it is a passage, not a place to stay. Surviving and living through grief is part of life, and ultimately it can contribute to:

- Growth and compassion
- Strength and integrity
- Acceptance and faith
- Coping better with adversity
- Improved relationships

In my most recent dream about Pepper, I was in a residential neighborhood of mostly small houses. I was out for a jog with my dog, who resembled a little of each of my prior dogs. I realized that I forgot the leash and was in a neighborhood where dogs require leashes. I kept calling my dog to stay close and to come back before running off into the yards of the houses we passed. We had turned around and were heading back when another larger dog came running towards us, who appeared friendly. The dog appeared a little smaller as it got closer. It checked us out, then ran back to where it had first appeared. I continued my run with my dog, with him being near and then running off and disappearing into the passing yards. I woke up.

I interpreted the dream as a reflection on mourning and losing my pet Pepper, who was now free and "off-leash" to return in my memories occasionally. Pepper, or my other prior dogs, would return less often in my thoughts over time, with each dream, and yet will always remain in my heart.

TIPS: WHEN GRIEVING LOSS OF A PET

Loss is painful, and it follows its unique course for each of us as we learn from the experience of grief, dying, and death. The process is a way of developing wisdom, acceptance, and the art of letting go. These are lessons from life and preparation for our aging and dying, and/or death of a significant other. If possible or appropriate for you, consider adopting another pet from the many awaiting an owner. Find positive ways of helping and giving your love, support, and spirit to others. It may profoundly change your life.

HURRICANES, TRAUMA,
AND RECOVERY

Mary* was a young single mother, divorced, living just above the poverty line, with a thirteen-year-old daughter. With her new server job, she moved into a small rental cottage near a scenic local river. It was the first time Mary felt some security and had a place to call her own. Her daughter quickly enrolled in a nearby school.

Then the hurricane came and took everything: the house and all of her belongings. Mary just barely escaped and made it to a local shelter with her daughter. They moved in with Mary's mother after making repairs to what had been an estranged relationship.

Mary had a history of mood swings, depression, anxiety, and PTSD from childhood sexual abuse. She grew up in a very chaotic and disruptive home, especially after her alcoholic father deserted her and her mother. She had experienced a difficult time growing up with parental neglect and physical and emotional abuse. Mary had post-traumatic stress disorder (PTSD) from early childhood trauma, which returned after the hurricane. Mary's life felt like a continuing hurricane, a storm of swirling negative thoughts and emotions, worse at night, contributing to nightmares and poor sleep. She felt despondent and had suicidal thoughts about taking her own life to escape the torment. There was a loss of pleasure in doing her usual activities, and she felt hopeless and isolated from others.

After the hurricane, sessions with a counselor trained in trauma work helped her gain insight and relief. Mary experienced profound insights into the vicissitudes of life and the greater context in which all things exist. She saw the possibilities in herself and others for choices, compassion, acceptance, redemption, and more profound healing. She realized that she was a survivor of the destructive hurricane and the devastating storm in her mind that affected her at all levels—body, mind, and spirit. Mary gradually built a more sustainable healing and recovery program with a nurturing support network.

The hurricane had dismantled Mary's tightly held and limiting beliefs and attitudes. The great storm, literally and figuratively, swept away non-essential mental and emotional debris, leaving her open to more remarkable inner change, redemption, and transformation. In the past, her life was a repetition of painful cycles, driven by addiction, mood disturbance, trauma memories, and self-destructive choices. Now there was hope and a sense of a new beginning.

(*Mary is not an actual person but a composite of people with similar problems.)

EXTREME CONDITIONS

Extremes challenge the strengths of anyone involved, exposing vulnerabilities, whether to infectious pandemics, hurricanes, or wildfires. A catastrophe of any sort can cause massive destruction of property, the economy, and displacement and disruptions of lives. The resulting trauma and loss can lead to mood and other psychological difficulties. The full impact of traumatic experiences forces people and communities into survival mode, often with damaging aftermaths. The recovery process, and the rebuilding of the personal self or property, begin as the crisis events pass. For some people, the aftermath of the crisis is a time of reflection, self-assessment, taking a new perspective, and possibly personal and community transformation.

As in the current pandemic, individuals who experience an unexpected loss or occurrence can have residual difficulties. Associated with the trauma and loss are emotional pain, depression, and post-traumatic stress symptoms. Mary's story highlights the challenging and sometimes treacherous journey from despair and loss to healing and recovery.

The eye of a hurricane is an area of calm in the middle of the storm's activity. Even when experiencing periods of well-being, stability, peacefulness, and spiritual reprieve, a person can still have unresolved, early life disruptions or trauma. Mary had dark forebodings that she would relapse back into the devastating experience of depression, PTSD, and drug addiction—back into the fury of the storm.

Unresolved issues, traumas, and worries, as well as fearful thinking, feelings of vulnerability, or lack of resources can contribute to emotional difficulties, especially when the individual is challenged by a new traumatic experience. Openness to receiving help encourages seeking of therapy and treatment. Most important in healing and recovery is finding the **peaceful center in the storm's heart—the portal to serenity, healing, and transformation.** The center is the placeless place of timelessness, a feeling of connection, love, non-resistance, acceptance, quietness, and peace.

An essential part of the healing journey begins in moments of freedom from emotional turbulence. Gradually, as part of the healing journey, there are more extended periods of being calm and centered. Greater ease becomes possible for resourcing the serenity state of an enlightened awareness.

Concentric rings surround the center in the mandala art of the East. The mandala appears like a storm or hurricane, which always has an eye or center. The ancient yogis described the eternal peaceful center as "satchidananda," the realm of enlightenment: being, consciousness, bliss, happiness, and truth. The bands of a hurricane, or the mandala rings, can represent mental or emotional contraction stages, turmoil, or suffering, which arise out of a calm originating center of all potentiality. The way of survival or healing is to come back to the place of sanctuary, spiritual connection, or respite. A movement towards the center, from any location in the concentric rings of human experiences, is healing and enlightening.

One must survive the outward destructive storm and get to safety; then, healing and recovery can begin. A peaceful center of serenity and calm is always available and present, even while the busy mental activity and life's demands are happening, much as a wave in a surging sea is forever a part of the ocean. Access remains open with awareness, acceptance, compassion, and love.

SLEEP AND RECOVERY

Discovering the calm hurricane center is like the depressed person dropping into a place of quiet, peacefulness, and rejuvenation. The peaceful center is free of busy mental activity and agitation. The three stages of sleep are comparable to the journey to the serene center of consciousness. The center of the hurricane, or the inner peace sought by the depressed person, resembles the third stage of sleep:[39]

1. The **awake state** is where the mind is engaged in its alert, reasoning, worrying, or agitated modes.
2. The **dream stage** of sleep is where there is less focus and ties to mental or physical reality. A person gets some rest in dream sleep. When agitated or disturbing, dream time is a poor rest experience—frequent experience in the trauma-related nightmares of PTSD.
3. The **deep sleep stage** is where a person returns to a peaceful and recuperative state, waking to feel refreshed and revitalized. It is akin to discovering the calm hurricane center.

A CENTER OF BEING

The mind falls short in the attempt to explain the very abstract ideas or concepts of love, beauty, spirituality, the universe, or infinity. The state of pure awareness or heightened consciousness is a movement *beyond* more literal, constricted definitions and narrow contexts. The shift is to the realm of an abstract, expanded context, moving from the known and knowable to the unknown and unexplainable—beyond names and definitions—where science is only now exploring this uncharted territory.

What that is, or what we are, goes beyond finite description or words. Rupert Spira relates that the spiritual center is an always existing presence and the consciousness that we continuously have. He likens it to watching a movie on a screen: the screen is always there, yet one becomes unaware of the screen as the attending mind only sees the drama. As in a dream, we become both the dream and dream character, losing the awareness of who we are.[40] In the famous spiritual classic *I Am That*, Nisargadatta, one of India's great modern sages, brings his audience to a clearer understanding of the mind, being, and existence.[41] David Hawkins, MD, explains different consciousness levels, reflecting the limitations, conflicts, struggles, and suffering because of limiting mind-ego and linear, literal thinking in a narrow context. The realization or enlightenment to truth becomes paramount to moving out of the containment, struggle, or entrapment of lower levels of ignorance, non-truth, and misunderstanding.[42] And for Jean Klein, the root of all desires is the one desire to come home to peace.[43]

THE OCEAN, PLACE OF WAVES, STORMS, AND HURRICANES

The ocean is a body of water and is also a metaphor in Eastern thought; it represents the underlying principle or origin of all things and appearances. Spiritual, religious, and Eastern philosophies support the idea of one central infinite creative source—the potential from which all perceived or experienced things originate. The works of Joseph Campbell and Carl Jung offer an in-depth examination of the human psyche, spirituality, myths, and symbols as water, the ocean, etc.[44]

Advanced scientists, mystics, and meditators often express the deeper meaning of the observed and experienced world:

- In Eastern thought, it is the all-encompassing infinite source, the self, and pure awareness versus the limiting mind-ego, "small self," inflexible patterns of beliefs, concepts, and perceptions.

- Yoga is a traditional practice from the East, which involves movement, stretching, holding postures, relaxed breathing, mindfulness, and finally resting quietly in peaceful repose.

- Meditation or prayer leads to a place of calm and peacefulness—a sanctuary from the emotional and physical anguish and excessive activation.

- The opposite point of view dominates in some Western, materialistic, or less advanced scientific thought. In these systems of thought, everything experienced in the perceiving, thinking mind exists only as an actual object or as solid matter.

OPENING TO LIFE AND HEALING

For good mental health, the ability to get to the centering moments—the "pauses," as finding the calm place during a storm—brings respite. The moments of calm can occur between thoughts and activities or after gratification of desire.

"Centering" helps people to regain flexibility and balance. There can be a lessening of rigid thinking patterns and intrusive, painful memories. Growing moments of liberation—from disturbing thoughts, images, and beliefs—builds a foundation for recovery.

In the hurricane's aftermath, or post-pandemic, comes the rebuilding process. For healing, more robust integration of mind, body, and spirit needs to occur. A lasting connection with the center of peacefulness, serenity, calm, unity, happiness, and love must become a reality. It creates stability and balance through the potent presence and connection with the tranquil center of consciousness.

TIPS: FINDING THE CENTER

- Find the time and ways to balance the busyness of the self-centered mind and of goal-oriented "practical" activity with non-attached awareness. Seek the experience of being in the peaceful center of unity-consciousness and connectedness with all that is outside of our separate self and identity. As obstructions or entrapment of the mind dissolve, there is a passage to moments of calm, peacefulness, and harmony.

- Balancing the individual, functioning self with the experience of being one with the moment brings a vastness, such as experiencing a beautiful sunset or a walk in a natural setting—as on a lovely ocean beach with the sun setting or rising—bringing the sense of timeless eternity, rapture, and infinite possibilities.

- Integrative-holistic guidance or mentoring can help facilitate recovery and a return to a healthy integration of mind, body, and spirit. Spiritual emergence-oriented programs recognize that many psychological distress symptoms, or life crises, represent an opening and opportunity for healing at a higher level of experiencing and functioning from a more enlightened awareness and consciousness.

- Using conventional medical or psychiatric labeling, diagnosing, and treatment, like the attention to symptoms, is only a starting point in the journey of healing and discovery. Spiritual emergence approaches use the analogy of the birth process and moving through the birth canal towards the light, liberation, life, and integration.[45]

- Regular attuning of the body with healthy practices is a good beginning, including improving lifestyle, exercise, and diet. Other essentials are everyday practices like meditation, self-reflection, or prayer. Companionship with persons and pets helps get past the individual mind and ego. Join or share with a supportive social network, for the power of recovery is often seen in the twelve-step programs in addiction recovery work.[46]

All those affected by the recent calamity of natural disasters, such as recent hurricanes, fires, and pandemics, need compassion and help. With the current catastrophic damage to so many people's lives and possessions, one can help by giving to charity and relief efforts.[47] Finding positive ways to help those affected with support, guidance, or therapy support, are an opportunity to help those in need.

COVID-19 AND POLIO PAST

In the summer of 1952, I was an active young boy, always hiking in the woods, swimming, and playing sports. I then developed high fevers and was bedridden for several days with headaches and a stiff neck. After a brief exam, the doctor told my family that I had polio and sent me to the children's hospital. The diagnosis shocked me. When my older brother began teasing me about it, after my initial doctor's visit, I yelled that it wasn't true. To me, getting polio was like a death sentence, as I had seen all the pictures of disabled children and iron lung respirators used in those days to keep people alive.

When I arrived in hospital as a terrified little kid, my first time away from home, the nurse said she would have the doctor put a long needle in my back to do a spinal tap. The nurse then left me shivering for a half-hour on a hard table until she returned with the doctor. The nurse held me tightly with my head draped over her shoulder during the procedure. Then I was transferred to a children's ward with twenty or more screaming, frightened children. I cried and was up most of the night, sick to my stomach and vomiting. When the morning came, I gave in to the experience. I then got a lot of care and attention from the medical staff and nurses, who explained that I was positive for polio.

I heard that I had the non-paralytic form (post-polio meningitis), that I was one of the lucky ones. I would still have to remain in the hospital for several weeks for further tests. While in the hospital, I would receive the day's standard therapy: Sister Elizabeth Kenny's hot pack therapy and physical therapy, including exercise in a heated pool. It was a natural treatment, and the only known, potentially helpful treatment at that time. In the early part of my medical career, I realized an association with the traumatic experience of my getting ill during the polio epidemic and the anxiety and panic attacks that I had developed.

EPIDEMICS AND PANDEMICS

The polio epidemic that peaked in the early 1950s, though caused by an entirely different virus, can give some insight into what could be the course of COVID-19. The great fear of this devastating disease was that it crippled thousands of previously active, healthy children and could cause respiratory distress, leading to dependence on a respirator for several months or even indefinitely. In the polio epidemics period, the iron lung was in use, an earlier form of more advanced respirators. This disease had no cure and no identified causes, plus its more severe conditions led to a high death rate.

FEARS OF BEING A POLIO VICTIM

In contrast to the survivors of other viruses and tuberculosis, the polio victims who developed paralysis had a lifetime of disability. The thought of being paralyzed, or worse, was terrifying, with images everywhere of disabled children in braces or on iron lung respirators. (More than 200,000 people in the U.S. remain affected by the poliovirus. According to the World Health Organization, polio survivors continue to be among the largest disabled group in today's world.)

As with COVID-19, public places were closed, and people isolated themselves. Many lived in fear of the constant threat of catching the disease. Other diseases, such as influenza, had much higher mortality rates but didn't cause the lasting paralysis that polio could. There were no effective control measures to stop polio spread, which peaked in the summer months, so swimming pools were often closed.

The polio epidemic was widely reported in the news. Sizeable national foundations developed, such as the National Foundation for Infantile Paralysis and the March of Dimes. The organizations became important in raising funds to pay for the expensive treatments and equipment needed for polio victims' rehabilitation and care. These organizations and philanthropic groups also helped to provide the research funding, research that eventually led to the Salk and Sabin vaccine that stopped polio and its spread.

My family was also aware of the horror and tragedy of viral epidemics. My mother had lost her 19-year-old brother Harry to the Spanish Flu outbreak in 1918. Harry had been one of my father's best friends (which was how my parents met). While the polio epidemics seemed to recur and worsen every summer, there was always the hope that the virus would miss us.

A recurring problem, then and now, is our lack of preparedness, available testing, and medical resources such as ventilators and personal protective equipment (now also needed in the COVID-19's wake). Until enough are vaccinated to reach herd immunity, severe illness, or death will depend on several factors. The crucial element under our control would be the level of social avoidance and distancing from carriers of the virus. The virus can enter through any gateways to our respiratory system (eyes, nose, and throat). As it is spread by close contact with another carrier of the virus, following recommended public health measures will be paramount. Necessary directives include avoiding touching contaminated surfaces, touching our faces, or inhaling the infective agent. Using sanitizers liberally—such as hand wipes, liquids, and sprays—is also essential.

WHAT'S NEW ON THE HORIZON WITH COVID-19?

Perhaps the most critical difference in the current pandemic is that science is more advanced, especially in isolating the infectious agent and in more rapidly producing effective vaccines. The current Emergency Use Authorized (EAU) vaccines, now being administered, will be available in the coming months to most people, especially to those at heightened risk. Our science and experience speeds both vaccine development and availability. A lot also depends on the virus activity and its characteristics, which we are now better understanding. Strict adherence to public health guidelines can help prevent COVID-19 infections and the development of more dangerous viral variants, thus protecting the vulnerable and unvaccinated.

Scientists are looking at treatments used during the polio epidemic, like passive immunization, and convalescent antibodies, where someone ill with the COVID-19 infection receives the plasma of someone recovering from the illness, rich in antibodies against the virus. Some older drugs are also being studied for their potential to slow the virus's entry into and spread in the body.

A new rapid diagnostic test for COVID-19 is now available with quicker results. Plans are being made to mass-produce the test and make it more accessible. More aggressive public health measures, such as contact tracing, also appear to help contain and to prevent future outbreaks as well.

LOOKING AHEAD

Hopefully, as in influenza and polio epidemics, our experience will help in the future. Currently, the county is far behind the curve in being prepared for the many recent cases within our borders. Our failure came from the unknowns about the novel virus itself and from the inadequate preparedness and leadership on multiple government levels. Our country is also behind through not having an adequate strategic reserve of hospital beds, respirators, personal protective equipment, and other vital resources and personnel.

Today, many infectious diseases experts believe that we can't let our guard down again and so be unprepared for the next new virus, as our county and most other world governments were with COVID-19. Unpreparedness has also been the problem with many prior epidemics. The warning is that nature can always be one step ahead of us, and that novel forms of viruses are ever-developing and waiting to become the next epidemic or pandemic.[48]

THE ELEPHANT IN
COVID-19'S ROOM

With their occasional relationship difficulties, Peter and Sarah had been reasonably successful in their respective long-term recovery programs for substance use. Peter had been doing well for many years in a medication assisted treatment program for his narcotics addiction. As a help for their health, well-being, and relationship, they had developed a daily practice of study, meditation, and prayer. Sarah felt they were "walking the walk" not just "talking the talk" of recovery. Both acknowledged the challenge of each taking a different approach to substance use disorder recovery, with Sarah following an abstinence-based 12-step model of recovery and Peter doing a medication-assisted program with methadone. They followed integrative and holistic practices to sustain themselves, their relationship, and their personal recovery paths.

Unforeseen challenges entered the picture during the pandemic, with the added pressure in their work and being bottled up in their residence with the demands of social isolation. They also had to avoid many of the stress-reducing social activities that had been available before COVID-19. Even with the added tensions of living and negotiating relationship demands in a small space, Peter moved ahead with treatment for Hepatitis C to heal his liver. Beyond the emotional and physical difficulties of the treatment, his overall health seemed to return.

But other noticeable changes became more prominent, such as difficulty sleeping, increasing irritability, and physical discomforts. Peter reported vague, bothersome, sometimes scary "romancing the drug" thoughts, and subtle cravings. As more frequent and occasionally near-violent arguments ensued, they thought, with all the pressure of COVID-19 and what felt like increasing incompatibility, their relationship wouldn't make it and was nearing the end.

When they could get out and walk, the bigger picture unfolded about what had been out of their awareness in the recent months' turmoil and distress. In trying to navigate the turbulence of what seemed to become an intolerable relationship, much of importance had been missed. Some simple realities emerged: the combinations of factors such as Peter's liver treatment and all the stress of COVID-19 had shifted the need for regulation of methadone.

Peter immediately contacted his MAT treatment program, and his methadone was adjusted, which brought him back to a stable state. Peter and Sarah resumed with more vigor their meditation and health-enhancing programs. Their relationship returned to a healthy flow with minimal conflict. Now they both recognized the need, when pressure mounted, and tempers flared, to look for the often hidden and subtle factors, and not to get caught up in the moment's passion, but to relax back in that deeper place of clarity, mindfulness, acceptance, and love. (Of course, a little bit of a detached, objective, scientific mind is always helpful as well.)

Sarah also had the insight that one shouldn't lose awareness of the subtle or sometimes drastic changes that can occur in our lives, of the need to be more fluid, aware, and ready for change, for adaptation, and growth. She felt their relationship had hit some real turbulence, but that now, with increased mindfulness and awareness, they were better prepared for a new day with an open mind and heart.

(*Peter and Sarah are not an actual couple, but a composite of people with similar issues encountered in the past and more recently during the COVID-19 pandemic.)

WAKING UP TO THE HIDDEN TRUTHS

Truths and reality can be lost in the personal travails of everyday life and relationships. Challenges and difficulties get magnified (or sidelined) during the demands and stresses of the COVID-19 pandemic or any other crisis. Sarah and Peter were doing all the right things—physically, mentally, spiritually, and health-wise—during the pandemic, but missed the elephant that almost unraveled their relationship.

Similarly, the blindness to or the missing of critical facts, like the spinning away from "inconvenient truths" in the current COVID-19 crisis, represents a great danger to our safety, well-being, and survival. In business and politics, controlling the narrative merely to win customers, build a brand, or gain a captive audience of followers, can *seem* like the way towards profits or power. In reality, people's awareness and attention, unfortunately, gets diverted away from critical issues that need action. Not attending to these vital issues is a formula for economic disaster and a recurrence of tragedies like the deadly pandemic.

A NEW LEVEL OF FOCUS IS NEEDED

Even at the height of the U.S. COVID-19 catastrophe, charitable intent in politics seems to be lacking. Other people assume that everyone in a crisis pulls for the common good and that altruism prevails. Still, others ignore science, blame others, or promulgate conspiracy theories and false narratives. There may be an attempt to "dumb down" data for the population or to keep people away from the truth, accurate information, and education in certain respects. The susceptibility to additional, disruptive social or political changes often occurs.

Extreme weather and coastal flooding are also potential factors in the cause of new, deadly viral agents and pandemics that could contribute to the increased susceptibility of populations to disease. For instance, massive storms and droughts have displaced large populations, contributing to migration, poverty, and more people seeking refuge. Displaced people often end up in unsanitary, densely populated neighborhoods, with compromised food supplies and a lack of available medical services.

Social scientists and governments have significant concerns about overpopulation, and the march of technology is proceeding faster than it can be understood and managed. Overpopulation, growth, and technology with automation will continually contribute to more scarcity of employment and loss of jobs. Such changes also would lead to more concentration of wealth and of resources in the hands of a smaller number of individuals, large businesses, and manufacturers.

All told, the failure of government, public services, leadership, scientists, and industry has been in the inadequate preparation for epidemics or pandemics of current proportions. So far, there has been a lack of global cooperation and/or consortium-building to develop and manage the occurrences of pandemics or international crises. What appears to be needed are better methods and technology to produce vaccines more rapidly and to have considerable reserves of necessary health care materials, resources, and equipment.

HEALTH DISPARITIES CAN CHANGE OUTCOMES

The coronavirus has caused an excessive mortality and death rate in minority, disadvantaged, or non-privileged communities. The virus appears to be more deadly in people made vulnerable by the underlying health issues prevalent in minority populations. Increased numbers of at-risk people are likely among people of color, immigrants, and individuals living at or below poverty levels. Other contributors to poor outcomes would be the lack of access to quality healthcare and medication, higher unemployment, racism, overcrowding in housing, and/or living in higher-density parts of urban areas. The localities where these at-risk populations live often experience more pollution and a closer proximity to factories or other contamination sources.

Several health conditions might contribute to more severe illness and death from COVID-19. A list of frequent contributors would include immune deficiencies, cancer, heart disease, undiagnosed infections, obesity, inadequate diet, nutritional deficiencies, smoking, drug addiction, untreated mental illness, people on multiple medications, respiratory ailment, asthma, lung disease such as COPD, diabetes, hypertension, and increased infirmity, such as is seen in older adults. There has also been an exceptionally high death rate in nursing homes. Many elderly residents have compromised health conditions and live in high-density units, with sometimes marginal care, poor nutrition, and lack of physical activity.

Severe illness and death in the vulnerable bring up the major public health issues that have not received attention and priority for governmental and public programming and funding. The opioid epidemic is an extreme example of what can happen because of limited access to effective treatment options.

Solutions are more likely with the help of informed leaders and a focus on identified critical problems. Public attention seemed to improve the high rates of lung disease, cancer, and COPD with better control of tobacco products and pressure on the industry to curb its product marketing. Improvements in asthma rates began in the 1970s with the development of smog reduction programs. (Now we have vaping, which needs scrutiny and increased public awareness.)

TIPS: POSSIBILITIES FOR ACTION

If more citizens and government leaders focus on the genuine issues and public health needs related to COVID-19 prevention or occurrence, what might be the immediate policy changes or interventions? The first would be to identify businesses and officials who deliberately distract or lead the public attention away from the critical issues. Instead, voters might support or influence community and federal leaders to direct government funding and programming to communities in need.

Reliable, informed, and committed leaders at the federal level will also be essential to provide adequate coordination of the local efforts and programs. For example, now that we have identified the communities at the highest risk for severe illness and death from the virus, let's set up services, health education, and medical resources for these specific areas and populations. Such efforts will require a focus on science and public health research.

Efforts would also include building up public health education, services, clinics, and hospital services in the high-demand and needy regions. For-profit hospitals, private medical practices, and facilities would team up with federal funding and public healthcare programs to bring about positive change.

Being inattentive or ignorant of situations that need remedies is a set up for another disaster, recurrent high death rates, and future pandemics. Let's keep our eyes and ears on the genuine issues and get our public leaders in line with national needs.

PART IV: BEYOND COPING

REDUCING DISEASE RISK
DURING TOUGH TIMES

In a dream, I was visiting a city with my wife, where we formerly lived. We stayed in a quaint bed and breakfast, where an older gentleman we knew was also staying. We all took a tour of the city's former fashionable section, where there were arty shops and various restaurants. I remembered this as a place to walk, browse, shop in the enticing small stores, and get a bite in one of the exotic eateries.

When we arrived after a brief drive, there was an eerie and decadent appearance to the formerly fashionable area and hang out. Stores and restaurants were boarded up. The streets and parking areas reflected derelict upkeep with trash scattered everywhere. We knew it was probably related to the devastation of the COVID-19 pandemic.

We got out of the car and walked towards a still-open shop and restaurant with a crowd of mostly younger people milling around the restaurant's doorway. I remembered that the COVID-19 pandemic was still raging, and yet none of the younger group of people had masks on. I became acutely aware that we were not wearing masks either. It immediately felt like a dangerous and threatening

*situation. I called to our group that we needed to get out of harm's way, go back
to our car, put on our masks, and leave the area.*

Waking up from that dream, I reflected on several things: how precarious
life can be if there isn't a high level of care and vigilance, and the necessity
to avoid risky situations or being forgetful in not taking all the precautions.
These precautions, of course, would include mask-wearing and avoidance of
high-risk situations, especially where the risk of exposure and infection is
high.

Dreams can inform and often reflect deeper truths and realities that
sometimes get lost in our busy day-to-day life activities. After waking up, I
scanned the news, and COVID-19 was continuing to ravage the country with
the highest number of deaths in a single day, and more hospitals were becoming
overwhelmed with the surge of new patients. There was the promising news of
help on the way with three new Emergency Use Authorization (EUA) vaccines
being made available for protection The headlines called for people to be
responsible and do their part in reducing the virus's spread. With the holidays,
many people planned to travel and gather anyway.

Now isn't the time to let down our guard, even with three vaccines available.
**In not recognizing the situation's gravity and need for continued precautions,
a surge in illness and deaths can occur. So pay attention to your dreams,
wake up, be aware, and act responsibly.** Let's consider some key questions for
challenging times.

HOW CAN I THRIVE IN THE COMING MONTHS?

In a pandemic, information changes daily. The threat of severe health
impairment, mood impairment, or even death brings up many questions
and concerns. The pandemic continues as a frightening experience, with
much uncertainty and social unrest. Protests about issues our society and
government have failed to acknowledge or remedy creates more dread and

worry. A desperate and frightened person might seek answers to their current perplexing, pandemic-related situation by seeking updated information, a fresh perspective, or searching for support and reassurance. Are there practical things we can do for safety and greater peace of mind? What steps will ensure a better personal and family future? How can one be a part of the solution rather than part of the problem?

Response: Many proactive steps can speed the end to the pandemic and support needed changes:

- To protect health and well-being, keep up-to-date with the latest news and recommendations from reputable, varied sources (such as established news networks, publications, and the CDC). Keep your guard up. Even though vaccines are now available with people getting vaccinated, the concern is still with the spread and infection of unvaccinated or vulnerable individuals to the persisting virus or variant viruses that might circumvent the vaccine.

- Be careful to avoid any politically-motivated misinformation.

- The other needed ingredient is active local, state, and national efforts to provide adequate protective gear for those in risky exposure settings; testing; contact tracing emergency services; and essential support for food, shelter, and financial needs.

- The vulnerable groups for whom COVID-19 can be a deadly illness need to avoid crowding or close contact in enclosed spaces, especially where people are not wearing masks and not remaining socially distant. Those vulnerable to life-threatening infections would include obesity, diabetes, smokers with chronic respiratory disease, blood type A, kidney, cardiovascular (heart) disease, low vitamin D levels, and immune deficiencies. Any exposure to the virus can cause a significant COVID-19 infection.

- Maintain social distancing of at least 6 feet.

- Avoid being enclosed with groups of people. Occurrences of the illness can happen when in close contact for any length of time in a closed space, even with asymptomatic carriers of COVID-19, or with those who are coughing, sneezing, yelling, screaming, and not wearing masks or socially distancing.

- Medically challenged individuals in nursing, rehab, hospitals, or extended-care facilities will need to follow the strictest public health guidelines. Loved ones and healthcare providers need to be vigilant at all times to ensure that the utmost caution is observed.

- Anytime you can change your lifestyle, as when seeking improved nutrition, not smoking, losing excess weight, or exercising regularly, your risk of infection diminishes. Get accurate information from healthcare experts, health coaches, reliable online or TV sources, and classes. Do whatever you can to move in a definite health improvement direction.

- To get more effective leadership and policymakers, get useful information from non-partisan sources, and support the leaders you feel will make a difference.

- Anytime you're going to spend time near someone who is not part of your household, wear a mask, both indoors and outdoors. It would be best if you spent minimal time in indoor spaces with non-household members.

- Move any activities outdoors whenever possible. Vitamin D from outdoor activity and sunshine has potential protective benefits. Many dying from COVID-19 have low Vitamin D levels.

- Remember to wash your hands frequently. Isolate yourself, especially if you feel any exposure as per public health guidelines, and stay home away from others if you feel sick.

- Contaminated surfaces may also spread the infection. Hence, it is essential to use sanitizers and wipes to decontaminate any exposed area and to do frequent handwashing.[49]

TIPS: WHY WEAR A MASK?

Masks and physical (social) distancing require strict adherence while the pandemic continues to spread and endanger the most vulnerable lives. Also, not wearing masks or not taking other steps such as physical distancing prolongs the shutdown of our economy. Any encouragement *not* to follow the public health guidelines from the influential voices in government and the community simply enables the virus to spread, along with its deadly impact on those unable to defend themselves.

Masks protect you from anybody who may breathe, cough, or sneeze near you, or who is present in a closed space or poorly ventilated room with you. And remember: **many spreaders of COVID-19 are asymptomatic and are unaware that they are carrying the virus.** The mask may provide some protection for you. To provide a higher level of safety, if you're in a vulnerable risk category or high-risk social situation, wear the type of mask that offers a higher level of protection, such as an KN-95 mask. Wearing a mask is an essential part of the control of infection or contagion and of the prevention of infection in others and yourself, especially when you can't maintain a six-foot distance.

WILL I BE AT GREATER RISK?

Will I be more at risk for COVID-19 or a recurrence of mood problems if I have suffered from anxiety and depression in the past?

Response: Most experts feel that if you are prone to depression and anxiety, or have suffered it in the past, you will be at higher risk of recurrent mood or anxiety problems, especially during or after the pandemic.

The pandemic situation creates a pressure cooker effect with mounting stresses and anxieties, especially when society shuts down to limit contagion, doing without the usual social support, connection, and recreational activities to "let off steam." The closed-in situation, reduced exercise, and avoidance of public places lead to increased poor nutrition, weight gain, diabetes, and other chronic degenerative health conditions. New onset or a recurrence of significant anxiety or depression can cause a vulnerable state and possibly increase the risk of acquiring or having more severe consequences from a viral illness. **If signs and symptoms of depression or anxiety surface, seek a mental health specialist or a practitioner's advice and treatment.**[50]

PANDEMIC LIFE SAVERS

WISE CHOICES

To ensure a safe journey through crises and the pandemic's present hazardous times, make wise choices. Be vigilant to protect yourself and others from one of the most virulent and dangerous viruses in U.S. history. Keep tuned to the latest news and recommendations from reputable sources, but be careful to avoid any extreme or politically motivated misinformation. COVID-19 infections and spread will continue until effective anti-viral drugs, vaccines, adequate testing, and contact tracing are available to all. Now that safe and effective vaccines are available, the work at hand is achieving adequate supplies, distribution, and administration to curb COVID-19 infections and the pandemic. Experts believe that these new vaccines will eventually end the pandemic.

To repeat critical information from the previous chapter: those at higher risk for life-threatening infections are people with conditions as obesity, diabetes, smokers with chronic respiratory disease, kidney, cardiovascular (heart) disease, and immune deficiencies. Those vulnerable persons for whom COVID-19 can be a deadly illness and all potential spreaders of the virus need to **avoid closed, poorly ventilated spaces**, whether or not people are wearing masks and social distancing.

TAKE STEPS TO SUSTAIN HEALTH AND ENDURANCE

Our population has experienced a significant increase in anxiety, depression, illnesses, and death. Such emotional distress and mental impairment can cause loss of work time, disruptions in relationships, drug addictions, and suicidality, aggravating the pandemic's economic and social impacts. Early recognition, getting support and help, is critical for preventing and reducing the risk for chronic emotional and mental impairments and related physical illnesses.

When severe and recurrent fear and anxiety persist, relief can be possible with adequate support and help. Guidance and therapy can be useful to:

- Reduce or eliminate anxiety, panic, addictions, and trauma-related issues
- Be more present, mindful, and aware.
- Improve sleep, calmness, energy, focus, concentration, and daily functioning
- Develop greater acceptance and compassion
- Regain the wisdom and the balance of personal power, self-needs, and the needs of others
- Reestablish social support and networks

Therapies for anxiety, mood impairments, and prior trauma can also reduce stress and anxiety. Helpful therapeutic interventions—such as those with holistic, humanistic, or transpersonal approaches–can provide:

- Education about the body's physiological reaction to fear and threat
- Experiential, talk/listening, person-to-person, or group therapies
- Desensitization to the various physical sensations or triggers of anxiety/panic through the exposure of a person to the actual anxiety-provoking objects, situations, or thoughts
- Catastrophic-thought-reducing techniques
- Improvement in relaxation breathing; stress, anger, conflict

management techniques; and social interaction skills

- Restructuring of dysfunctional thoughts, beliefs, and patterns
- Personal insights and realizations of one's inner strength to overcome obstacles
- The transformations from being the victim of horrible traumatic experiences and memories to a broader perception of life, one's power, and potentialities
- Acceptance that the mind/body is continually moving toward the healing of its own emotional and mental health difficulties
- Commitment to the healing process and therapeutic work
- Support for the release of frozen past traumatic memories and constricting defenses to regain energy flow and vitality
- Help for recovering flexibility, getting unstuck from rigid core beliefs and attitudes
- Expansion of vision and perspective beyond the narrow constraints of a limiting mind-ego (the learned, cultured, molded self that strongly influences our life experience)

UNDERLYING EFFECTS

Healthcare providers are often not familiar with the potentially devastating effects and disability caused by the improper care of anxiety-related conditions. Management of anxiety done with a tranquilizer, an antidepressant, or reassurance by conventional healthcare practitioners is often insufficient. A thorough evaluation by a qualified medical and mental health practitioner with skills and expertise in working with anxiety, panic, and mood difficulties, is often warranted, helpful, and a better route when available. Finding caring and valuable assistance, when possible, may get at the deeper issues and the roots of anxiety or mood conditions.

Medication may be of value in resistant or severe emotional or mental health conditions, like major depression, if more natural therapies have not been effective. Antidepressants or tranquilizers are often used by conventional medical practitioners and sometimes bring more immediate relief. However, their long-term use is controversial, with the concern for their potential to cause other medical issues. Trying to stop medication can lead to relapse, or, with some tranquilizing drugs or alcohol, can cause withdrawal symptoms or seizures. Finally, pills may not have the same lasting effect and benefits as therapy programs and the use of natural alternatives.

Holistic and natural therapies can be the most effective treatment course when combined with more traditional treatment. Some positive complementary approaches for consideration are:

- Lifestyle modifications and life skill enhancements
- Mind, body; and spiritual practice as yoga, chi gong, mindfulness, meditation, creative arts, breathwork; and exercise with mindfulness as running, swimming, biking, or dance
- Stress management and relaxation techniques
- Acupuncture and massage therapies
- Targeted nutritional therapies, botanical medicine, and nutritional education about dietary choices and micronutrients (as herbs, vitamins, minerals, healthy fats, and protein)

TIPS: ADDITIONAL HEALTH GUARDS

Please review the helpful tips presented on pg. 15 for ideas on wellness.[51]

VULNERABLE HOSTS
AND A WAY FORWARD

ABC Co., a large corporation, hired a new leader for their marketing and management department. As part of their corporate policies, any new hires to critical positions with high levels of responsibility and visibility had to undergo a complete evaluation and testing by a well-respected recruiting firm, which did very sophisticated and scientific psychological reviews.

The recruiting firm's report on the new hire uncovered strengths: the potential employee had a fantastic ability to gain people's trust and liking, was a natural sales agent, and was good at self-promotion. However, the report also enumerated at least one failed business, three failed marriages, and only lukewarm personal and professional references. The extensive psychological testing by a psychologist specializing in organizational development and human resource work reported several other red flags, including results in the highly probable range for a long-standing personality disorder.[52]

However, Bob, the CEO, was suspicious of testing and data, surrounding himself with others who felt the same way. And so, after glancing at the report from HR, the hiring team went with their initial gut instincts, visions of dollar signs dancing in their heads.

After six months, the new hire went on "administrative leave" because of several complaints about inappropriate sexual comments. Next came customer complaints about his misleading marketing and fabricated stories. The CFO then discovered questionable accounting. Finally, the new hire was influential in scuttling a company-wide policy to address the dangers of the new COVID-19 virus; the company lost many employees to infections, put their customers at risk, and faced yet more lawsuits, this time brought by federal agencies.

Bob's mild obesity, hypertension, lack of a healthy diet, a sedentary lifestyle, and the increasing stress of his corporate role had put him at risk for a COVID-19 infection–as did the lack of policies to protect him in his workplace. Fortunately, his family doctor took preventative steps at the first signs of illness. Bob spent several days in the intensive care unit with oxygen and other treatments.

His eyes opened, Bob returned home and retired, and the company recruited a new CEO, a person with years of executive experience at a slightly smaller company that had grown and become very successful. This time, the hiring team paid close attention to the expert's assessments and hired a new marketing head. She was very personable and forward-thinking, yet also analytical, and she paid close attention to the details and advice of knowledgeable leaders in her field. As a result, the company could recoup its credibility and doubled its marketing presence and sales over the next year—all without additional lawsuits.

(*Bob is not an actual person but a composite of people with similar stories encountered in the past, presented for educational purposes only.)

WORST-CASE SCENARIO OF VICTIMS AND VULNERABILITIES

COVID-19 appears to have favorite human hosts as its preferred place to live, thrive, and infect. Control of such a highly contagious viral illness is unlikely, especially in the short-term, as universal compliance with social distancing and other precautions has been erratic. With time, individuals' desire to get out and return to more usual ways of life, work, or social activities could lead to less use of voluntary precautions. In a worst-case scenario, the breakdown in mitigation and social distancing strategies will happen due to several factors. The younger part of the population may especially feel invulnerable. Those who follow the news may decide that there is little risk for themselves. Communication that favors or tolerates misplaced, selfish motives may override the need for personal and social safety and well-being. Others might even begin to "blame the victim," involving the belief that innocent victims of the virus were somehow more dispensable or deserving of their fate. However, things do not have to be this way.

BEST-CASE SCENARIO OF SOLUTIONS AND PREVENTION

"An ounce of prevention is worth a pound of cure."

- Benjamin Franklin

What can science tell us to prevent future infections and recurrences of deadly viruses? The likely solution and prevention will come when a safe and effective vaccine becomes widely available and is used by a significant part of the population. Shorter-term help with the COVID-19 crisis will be possible through public health recommended practices, such as wearing masks and social distancing strategies. The other steps will probably include developing new treatments, either using older or newer drugs, and better coordination between testing, tracing, and interventions. Having adequate testing, personal protective (PPE) supplies, contact tracing, and the teaching of prevention will be critical. Finally, the lessons learned could lead to better planning and medical infrastructure for future preparedness.

Considering both scenarios, what risk factors—whether emotional, physical, or societal—must we address as a society to position us for health and resiliency over the coming months? Some considerations include avoiding the rejection of valid scientific information; nutrition, obesity and smoking; factors that create a virus host; threats to general health and well-being; and environmental risks.

AVOID THE REJECTION OF VALID SCIENTIFIC INFORMATION

Some segments of the population reject scientific information and follow practices contrary to the greater public welfare. Others focus on blaming or circulating conspiracy theories about others. In the fray, actual risks and immediate issues get ignored. Rather than focusing on the real enemy—disease—hostility is sometimes vented at "the messengers" tasked with delivering information or policies: the scientists, government members (especially the opposing political party), or others attempting to organize community action.

NUTRITION, OBESITY, SMOKING, AND COVID-19

Obesity and smoking are a significant risk for COVID-19 illness and the making of a more vulnerable host, with more substantial potential for severe disease and a higher death rate. Diseases related to poor nutrition, sedentary lifestyle, and obesity contribute to increased illnesses and higher death rates. Now the same is being found true for COVID-19 risk.

According to a recent article in *The New York Times*, "Obesity Linked to Severe Coronavirus Disease, Especially For Younger Patients," abdominal obesity, which is more prominent in men, can cause compression of the diaphragm and lungs and reduced chest capacity. Also, abdominal obesity can increase inflammatory instigators, which may contribute to the worst COVID-19 outcomes. The New York University Langone study found that patients under the age of 60 with obesity were at twice the risk for hospitalization and were at higher risk of requiring critical care. The same adverse consequences were not prominent in patients over the age of 60.

ADVERSE FACTORS CREATE INDIVIDUAL HOST VULNERABILITIES

Any person can become an ideal "host" for a microbe through their activities or characteristics. For example, any adverse condition or practice such as smoking or vaping compromises the lungs and increases respiratory viruses as COVID-19.[53] Other possible related contributors could be higher air pollution or living near polluters, such as specific factories. Preexisting health conditions or adverse socio-economic influences contribute to a higher potential for exposure, risk, or complication to many illnesses, including COVID-19.

Other factors or underlying medical problems and contributors include:

- Respiratory and chronic obstructive airway disease, obesity, diabetes, hypertension, kidney disease, cardiovascular disease, and immune deficiencies
- Opioid, drug, alcohol or other substance use disorder
- Being a member of a minority group, such as Black or Latino individuals, and living in a less affluent or less privileged community
- Inadequate education and limited job opportunities in more impoverished areas, where there is less access to health-promoting foods, medical care, and opportunities for recreation and exercise
- Nutrition illnesses related to a less active lifestyle, such as obesity, hypertension, and heart disease
- Global warming and climate change with increase catastrophic storms, flooding, and droughts
- More scarcity of food, related to issues like over-population, homelessness, crowding into high-density living areas, and ravages of war with the migrations of populations looking for safe haven
- Limited or no employment opportunities, including technological advances outpacing employee knowledge or management, with more job loss related to increasing automation

While all these factors are not "medical" per se, they all influence the ability to fight off or withstand infection.

THREATS TO GENERAL HEALTH AND WELL-BEING

Facts and science have identified significant threats to our community and the nation's health and well-being for many years before the current crisis. These simmering issues might have been underlying host factors that contributed to a person becoming the preferred target for an infective virus. Having *many* vulnerable hosts or potential victims in a population may be the critical cause of the high rate of contagion, the severity of illness, and deaths from COVID-19. The required focus and targeting of resources for improvement or resolution of the already-identified critical problems gets ignored or pushed to the "back burner." Other priorities or agendas have often led the efforts away from all these areas of urgent need. Decisions become influenced by shifting public opinion, political and special interest groups, businesses, governmental agencies, and their leaders. There has also been the "non-attention" of the people not directly affected, who get more focused on the maintenance or protection of their self-interests.

ENVIRONMENTAL RISKS

Limited or no access to clean water, healthy soil, or clear air generates its own set of health challenges. As trees are cleared and the ground dries up or erodes, entire populations can be weakened or displaced. This unstable situation makes it nearly impossible to coordinate a response to acute threats such as a pandemic. And yet, the facts, valid information, and research on these risks can get buried, ignored as irrelevant.

Years ago, Al Gore reviewed the science on global warming and warned about the rapidly approaching dangers and pending calamity for the planet. In his book *An Inconvenient Truth*, he presented how various segments of the population, political groups, and significant business interests dismissed what they saw as not relevant to their interests. Today, even with the steady progression of extreme weather and global warming with devastating storms, droughts, and coastal flooding, the science is still ignored by significant segments of our national and international community.[54]

Today, much of our population are consumers of misleading marketing information and deceptive advertising to promote a materialistic culture. Spun stories influence the behavior of targeted segments of our people. **Social media companies have gained a mastery of social psychology and the brain's response to stimuli. They have mined information on subscribers' consumer behavior, furthering their ability to influence those consumers. Behavioral and emotional manipulation, adherence to negative beliefs against fellow citizens and society fuel the current, angry political, and partisan divide, thereby generating further inaction to safeguard our precious resources.**

THE PATH FORWARD (OPTIMISM, OR WISHFUL THINKING?)

A crisis can also be an opportunity. In time, well-being and prosperity, the proverbial light at the end of the tunnel, will reemerge. People may then wake up to the essential issues and find opportunities for growth and healthy change. Besides a return to better mental health, there is also hope that the COVID-19 experience will bring a resurgence in interest in a healthy lifestyle, nutrition, exercise, environmental and spiritual attunement.[55]

ADVERSITY, REVELATION, AND OPPORTUNITY

A FORMIDABLE FOE

COVID-19 emerged as a new, frightening, and dangerous respiratory virus with many deaths because of a lack of immunity and natural protection. The deadly virus has already had a devastating impact globally and has taken an enormous toll on the lives of vulnerable individuals and communities. The combination of legitimate worries and fear, and the divisive nature of our partisan politics, have sometimes hindered the hoped-for progress and positive remedial steps. Mixed attitudes and conflicting responses have been commonplace in our communities. The present major economic crisis is comparable with the worst downturns our county has experienced. Everyday fears are about basic things: putting food on the table, unemployment, and adequate money to support oneself or one's family.

As with any natural or human-made disasters, a time comes for gradual containment, mitigation, rebuilding, healing of wounds, and revelation of deeper truths and knowledge to ensure a better and safer future. Scientists and citizens alike are waiting for the COVID-19 pandemic to subside, and there is hope for viral control with vaccines or antiviral drugs. While there is optimism for these treatments in the coming months, the dates are hard to predict. When a significant percentage of the population develops antibodies to the infection by vaccine immunization or exposure, the virus will have fewer vulnerable people to infect. Even when a substantial reduction in infections eventually occurs, such diseases may reappear at a future date, or new strains may develop.

Regardless of the specifics of the disease's course, unifying, focused leadership is essential for healing—from the pandemic, societal division, and partisanship. Otherwise, in a crisis like COVID-19, the public can become more divided as the fear of infection and death intensifies. Trying to resolve the many systemic problems becomes increasingly difficult if more people become swayed by the propaganda from the special interest groups looking for an advantage in a crisis. As a result, the safe reopening of society and our economy could be inadvertently sabotaged.

REMEMBERING LESSONS LEARNED

If we cannot learn from history, people will return to actions that created the conditions for a pandemic crisis. For example, we know that the increased risk for infection and severe illness arises from poor health, adverse lifestyles, and poor nutrition, contributing to many chronic debilitating conditions that make people more susceptible to infectious agents. Yet knowledge about the issues and problems does not ensure behavioral change.

The lack of social cohesiveness, cooperation, and mutual respect allows for increased division and partisanship. But when unified and cohesive work at prevention and action occurs, the risk of future vulnerabilities to sickness and pandemics decreases. From now on, everyone's ability to become better partners with the environment and with our fellow creatures will be paramount.

TIPS: TOWARD CONSTRUCTIVE ACTION

At the level of individual action, there is a need for:

- Improved personal healthcare, including mental health hygiene, exercise, nutrition, and lifestyles
- Lessening of obesity, smoking, hypertension, diabetes, and other chronic diseases[56]

At a societal level, we can work toward awareness or elimination of practices that create pockets of vulnerability, such as:

- Discriminatory practices
- Racism
- Economic disadvantage and income disparity
- Reduction of population density and overcrowding
- Unequal access to community resources, healthcare, and jobs, especially in economically depressed areas

Global and geopolitical action could focus on reducing long-term risk factors, including:

- Climate change and global warming
- Displacement of populations because of severe droughts, or megastorms such as hurricanes with coastal flooding
- Prevention of internal and international political conflicts—wars bring displacement, pain, hardship, and suffering to large parts of the world's population

A UNIFIED SEARCH

Currently, all eyes are on progress toward safe and effective vaccines. This heroic search for a vaccine is reminiscent of the polio epidemic in the past. As time passes, unfortunately, there may be individuals or groups of people who do not use vaccines. Many reasons surface to rationalize the non-use of vaccines recommended by the medical, science, and public health community. Some concerns may have merit, such as documenting adequate testing trials, but often refusals come from false or exaggerated misinformation.

Non-use of recommended vaccines can lead to the recurrence of contagion and severe consequences for the vulnerable, as seen in repeats in some geographic areas of measles, smallpox, and polio. With a new vaccine, a growing number of non-users could contribute to higher contagion rates and the development of more dangerous viral variants. Or many people could use the vaccines in the short run but later refuse them. As we've seen in similar situations, hospitals often protect vulnerable patients, staff, and healthcare workers by requiring that all employees get vaccinated for the flu every year.

MEETING THE INCREASED NEED FOR MENTAL HEALTH SERVICES

As presented in this book, catastrophes lead to a marked increase in the need for mental health services, particularly to treat trauma-related illness and mood disorders. The experience from prior pandemics and environmental catastrophes show that a significant portion of the population experiences anxiety, depression, and post-trauma conditions. Sufferers of preexisting mental health conditions, such as anxiety-related conditions, depression, or substance abuse, will be at risk for worsening of their problems during and after the crisis has subsided. As a result, the public needs better education regarding the signs and symptoms of mental health problems, as well as increased mental health services, especially in underserved communities. Expanding mental health resources will better serve us post-calamity or post-pandemic.[57]

OUR LEGACY

When we look back at this pandemic, let's hope that the legacy of COVID-19 will be:

1. Information and new scientific knowledge gained from the experience and study of the current viral pandemic

2. Increased public awareness about the positive impact of improving health practices, lifestyle, care of our environment, and appreciation and respect for differences

3. Improvements in medical and public health preparation and strategies to reduce the impact of future global health crises[58]

THE COVID-19
WAKE-UP CALL

My wife and I went out of the door of our house, fretting about the current pandemic, COVID-19 news, and the need for social distancing and mask-wearing. Suddenly, two black bears came bounding down the hill from the woods and stopped (as we did) in their tracks. It was a baby and her mother bear. We stood still, and the nearest to us, the baby bear, stood up to sense the air and to look in our direction. The cub then turned and followed his wise mother bear down the path away from us. The mother bear saw the threat and did the safe social distancing required to protect herself and her cub. I realized at that moment that we are all intimately intertwined with nature.

WAKING UP

Amid the current pandemic, although the viral threat is invisible, there are more telltale signs from nature and the natural environment. The bears are a reminder of how we can lose the close relationship with our surroundings' subtle warnings. **While life has become too complicated for many, all we need are the "bear" necessities, to use a pun.** The current COVID-19 pandemic or any catastrophe is a wake-up call to understand all the contributing factors and steps needed to protect ourselves and future generations from recurrences and devastation.

The martial law and strict enforcement around social distancing and quarantine in some Asian countries showed how a forced awareness could work. However, *an authoritarian government is not the desired outcome*. Instead, what learning, practical ideas, and wisdom will emerge from the pandemic experience? Our inquiry might focus on the following ideas:

- Individuals and society need better preparation and organization the next time an epidemic or pandemic occurs
- Refining our election process to fill critical governmental leadership positions with skilled, insightful, and experienced public servants
- Better preparation, production of vaccines, stockpiling of necessary health care resources and equipment
- The lack of leaders' and organizations' accountability and their failures to operate in the public interest
- Issues brought about by the march of technology
- A vital understanding regarding how our behaviors can contribute to imbalances in nature, which potentially unleashes destructive forces and pathogens

Optimistically, we will cultivate more profound respect for ourselves and others and recognize the intimate connection we all have to nature and to our own environment.

REAPING WHAT WE SOW

There is some truth in the old saying that we, as a people and a collective, will "reap what we sow." The term "karma" from Eastern thought and philosophy perhaps is also relevant. One interpretation of karma is that personal or collective actions will bring inevitable favorable or bad results.

Greed, selfishness, self-centeredness, fear, and feelings of being separate;

independent; or alone contribute to our fears of being vulnerable, not having enough, or lacking. The outcome can be submission or dependence on others, perceived authorities, institutions, or leaders. In the opposite direction, the same human tendencies can lead to the need to control or to dominate others, our environment, or resources. Conversely, to survive natural disasters or pandemics, it is essential to be socially aware and connected intimately with our environment. We need awareness and connection with all facets of life.

BEING IN AND OUTSIDE THE BOX–ALL AT ONCE

Overlooked aspects of our existence have been the pursuit of students, scientists, philosophers, theologians, spiritual seekers, and mystics. Even without the intentional search for this wisdom or understanding, many people have had profound experiences and realizations beyond personal knowledge and ordinary consciousness. Past cultures applied organized ways of benefiting from those extraordinary states beyond their usual everyday thinking and experiencing.

The value of such non-ordinary states of consciousness was beneficial for creative pursuits and achievements. Heightened states of wisdom and consciousness also benefited the leaders in warfare between tribes or during natural disasters. These meditative, non-traditional, experiential, and contemplative practices have often been a part of many cultures' shamanistic, tribal, religious, wisdom, or spiritual teachings. In our modern world, these expanded states of consciousness promote the balance between mental conflicts, dynamic thought processes, and serenity. The mind's essential peaceful, blissful, restorative, and open mode makes us more, rather than less, attuned to the state of our world.

Examples of some of today's forms of experiential and non-traditional therapies and practices are:
- Experiential-based individuals or group therapies
- Massage, bodywork, holotropic breathwork, yoga, meditation, and mindfulness

- Flotation tanks, sensory deprivation, and deep relaxation techniques
- Use of hallucinogenic drugs, sometimes called "visions quests," in some structured therapeutic settings
- Chanting, music, dance, and movement therapies
- Trauma-focused therapies for trauma sufferers
- Integrative or holistic therapies and techniques to facilitate healing
- Facilitation of non-ordinary states of consciousness and experiences to free the stifling effect of being stuck in constrictive mind space, especially if there has been a loss of spiritual perspective and connectedness

Unfortunately, many people confuse spirituality with religion or religious groups. Students of Eastern teachings, yoga, mindfulness, Buddhism, and modern holistic teachings typically do not seek adherence to religious practices but integration and connection to the mind, body, and spirit.

VALUE OF PRESENCE AND SPIRITUALITY

In a modern context, ancient traditions support man's search for meaning, wisdom, knowledge, happiness, and well-being in an ever-changing, unpredictable world of occasional disasters and pandemics. Welcome mental health benefits of being more connected to nature and spirituality would be:

- To be more constantly aware and present in the here and now
- The ability to more efficiently gain states of profound peace and relaxation—to access the feeling of connectedness, fulfillment, contentedness, and well-being
- To support human growth and potential, restorative, healing, and transformative experiences without the use of unnatural drugs and over-reliance on the sometimes excessive baggage of a religious sect or organization
- To enhance social connection and personal faith in one's own religious affiliations and organizations

The benefits of non-ordinary experiences, learning, and spirituality are well studied and are the basis for contemporary approaches to holistic, integrative health care, and psychotherapies.

RELIEF AND HEALING

As we deal with the current crisis and emerge from the pandemic, holistic and spiritual practices can bring comfort and healing to individuals and the present traumatized world. Despair over our tragic times can motivate all to become more aware, enlightened, and tuned in to the multitude of issues and needs of our greater society and environment. Now is the time to regain our more natural states of mindfulness, love, spirituality, and connection with others and our environment, versus being bound by excess self-absorption, greed, ignorance, and loss of contact with our true nature and reality.

AWARENESS OF DUALITY

There has been an awareness of duality in past times and civilizations, such as the way our minds compute or perceive things as distinct one way or the other. This is important as a basic need for survival, where our senses distinguish between safe or dangerous, good-tasting or toxic. It is the mental defining of the two sides of a coin, focusing on heads or tails, rather than the entire minted piece.

Focusing on the part rather than the whole may be essential for a routine life, safety, and decision making. It may be necessary to pick a winning team. Still, there is no winner in blind ignorance, hatred, and aggression, except for maybe giving an opening or advantage to a pathogen—a disease-producing agent—whether that is an aberrant virus or an ineffectual or dangerous political leader.

TIPS: SEEING THE WHOLE PICTURE

The way to prevent being caught in blind ignorance is by recognizing narrow-mindedness—also called "duality"—when not in touch with a higher level of awareness and consciousness. The higher level is shown in the ability to:

- See the entire reality of something while being able to sense the incompleteness of the apparent smaller components.
- Rise above the limitation of "small thinking," "narrow-mindedness," or biases.
- Work from a place of total awareness and acceptance of all the elements in the totality of a situation.
- Move forward with loving receptiveness for all involved.
- Be intuitive and use expanded creative thinking.
- Forgive the limitations or smallness in oneself and others.
- Compromise to serve the needs of both one's self and others.
- Be a faithful public servant, above narrow-minded partisanship and the jockeying for personal advantage or gain.

We can move toward embracing the whole and all the known elements to restore balance and integration.

OPPORTUNITY TO REGAIN BALANCE AND INTEGRATION

Many historical religious or secular movements, teachers, inspiring public figures, and sages came to the forefront during times of significant upheaval or calamities in societies, significant shifts in needs, and inadequacy of prevailing ways in supporting human life and institutions. In Judaism, Christianity, and Islam, there was the move from theology's dualistic nature to monotheism—embracing a higher organizing principle or power beyond human existence, conflicts, and limitations.

Living around the fifth century B.C.E., the Buddha illustrated the powerful shift in public attitude and direction in periods of turmoil and change. One aspect of the Buddha's teaching was gaining freedom from entrapments, tyranny of thoughts and senses, feelings, emotions, and perceptions. His followers hoped to gain the enlightening and transforming gift of non-dual experiential awareness and wisdom. In another example, Taoism was the Chinese teaching and philosophy of the benefits of modest actions, minimalism, and the value of a simple life close to nature. Confucianism was the teaching and philosophy of Confucius to be loving, treating others well, following moral and ethical ways, and not profiting from or taking advantage of others.

The opportunity in any tragedy, crisis, or cataclysmic events, such as the COVID-19 pandemic, can encourage new meaning and direction. The emergence of new traditions and influential movements arose in their turbulent times of need. Now is the time to expand our knowledge and consciousness beyond the fixation and imbalance of over-focus on our personal needs and dualistic self-oriented thinking.

Recreating balance in ourselves with all that exists in and outside of our individuality is the current challenge. The elevation into the non-dual or spiritual awareness and dimension has been what many prior generations of teachers and sages have sought to understand, master, and teach. **Now it seems such a time, when there appears to be a greater need than our technology, science, and political solutions offer. There is greater seeking of healthy alternatives to free up inflexible thinking and to prevent getting stuck in old ways; patterns; and rigid, destructive ideologies. The need to open up to the truth; wisdom; and understanding about the current disaster, its contributors, and the preventable steps to stop a future recurrence is the wake-up call of COVID-19.[59]**

EPILOGUE

It was a sunny, warm day in 1985, in the arid and desert-like landscape, when my wife and I walked into the modest hotel lobby near Jerusalem. We were to meet a newfound niece of my mother's dear cousin. We were young and full of wonder and adventure, excitation and anticipation that something profound would soon occur.

Several years before her death, my mother had expressed her regret for not finding her cousin during her one-time trip to Israel. The cousin had migrated there after her release from a Nazi concentration camp. The cousin, Iren, had corresponded with my mother, until she disappeared to the concentration camps. The Nazis had invaded her hometown in an area in Transylvania, near the Hungarian border. After the war, my mother's cousin, one of the few family survivors, wrote one last letter to my mother after migrating to Israel.

My mother had given me an addressed envelope received after World War II from Iren. My mother hoped that in the future I would find her beloved cousin and complete the connection for which my mother had wished. My mother remembered Iren as a small girl of her age, whom she had met when visiting their European family with her mother. After their visit, the two cousins kept in contact with an occasional letter.

Now, Iren's niece took us by car to the rustic lodging where Iren and her husband were staying. I had located Iren's niece by taking the envelope my mother had given me, with the old address and family name, to a multilingual shop owner. He took the time out from his work in his small stall-like shop to call twenty or so people with a family name similar to the one on my mother's envelope. He repeatedly told our story until Iren's niece recognized it. The shopkeeper was so sweet to help us, and of course, we bought a few gifts to remember him and his colorful shop.

When we walked into the room, Iren, who appeared slightly frail and elderly, with a concentration number tattooed on her arm, beamed with such warmth and a smile that our hearts melted, and all of us were crying and hugging. A profound sense of meaning came with the joining of our hearts and family past. The occasion was also profoundly moving, as just the day before we had visited the Holocaust Museum in Jerusalem. There were many reminders of that era's horrific events, such as the exhibit of thousands of children's shoes belonging to the many sent to the crematoriums by the Nazi's. Some of these children were of my mother's and Iren's family.

It was profound to meet Iren as a survivor of one of the worst tragedies in modern history. Iren had not only survived, but my impression was that she had moved to a much higher place of spirituality and love, though she still carried the deep scars of her losses and sacrifice. She had also become an accomplished poet and gave me some of the poems of her Holocaust experience, written in her native Hungarian, trying to find meaning in personal suffering and tragedy. When I returned to the states, I found a Hungarian professor who translated her poems.[60] My meeting with Iren reminded me of the writings of Viktor Frankl about his concentration camp experience and survival. His immortal book was Man's Search for Meaning.

This story brings to a close my writing and personal sharing about how everyone has had demanding or even catastrophic experiences, such as a crisis or tragedy, a life-changing event, or a significant loss. Any unpredictable life occurrence can trigger a deep search for meaning and purpose. **During these demanding times, we have to reach into our souls' depths, to adapt; survive; and regain our vitality, well-being, and spirit. The COVID-19 pandemic has been the upheaval, tragedy, and historic challenge of our time.**

COVID-19, THE PANDEMIC, AND THE FUTURE

A final reflection regarding the release of reportedly safe and effective vaccines, that has the potential of eventually bringing an end to one of the most deadly and destructive viral pandemics in history. As we look toward the end of the pandemic, let's dare to dream and to write an epilogue of hope:

In the pandemic, the U.S. and all the other countries of the world lost cherished and innocent beliefs about individuality, separateness, and independence. There was no security from a devastating, infectious pathogen, which quickly crossed permeable national boundaries. First, news reports from China alarmed the world of a life-threatening, novel virus, which was rapidly spreading and challenging to contain. Known as COVID-19, the contagious virus became a catastrophic global pandemic from the original origins, quickly moving between human hosts. The self-conceived bubble of safety and autonomy had burst into the reality of living in a global, interconnected population. One individual's impact could be sequentially spreading an infection to many others, and a series of missteps affected all the planet's health and well-being. As those tragic events passed, destruction, death, and loss became apparent. Healing came gradually with time, each individual dealing with the emotional impact of loss, grieving, and recovery in their own ways—and ultimately rebuilding meaningful lives.

AND THEN?

Gradually, with time, complacency again developed. There was a return to living back in a bubble of felt separateness and independence, a repetitive cycle fed by ignorance and self-interest. Indifference to the prevailing circumstances of the time, adversely affecting others, again prevailed ...

But wait—there is always the possibility for change, redemption, and transformation into a better future.

The remedy is the need for constant reminders to pay attention to the broader context and the world outside ourselves and to our internal emotional and mental experiencing and processing, whether turbulent, conflictual, loving, or serene. We must be always vigilant for unhealthy outside influences or adverse personal actions or behaviors. All must remember the dire consequences of not supporting and caring for ourselves, the environment in which we live, and others outside of our spheres of self-interest. Staying awake to the reality and truth of our existence and interdependence will remind us of the need for cooperation, acceptance, and co-existence. A holistic sensibility and awareness can be the guiding lights for mental health and the future of our planet.

For more information and continued learning, visit:
www.parksmd.com

ABOUT DR. PARKS

Dr. Parks is a respected physician, teacher, writer, and mentor with an integrative and holistic perspective. He is specialty-trained in internal medicine, nutrition, preventive medicine, and Board Certified in Psychiatry. Currently, Dr. Parks is the medical director and psychiatrist for The Center For Spiritual Emergence and Katharos Sanctuary (Intentional Longevity, Inc.) in Asheville, NC. Following a bout of polio in childhood, Dr. Parks received natural treatment, combined with the day's conventional treatments until his health returned. This illness and successful treatment experience gave him a deep respect for the combined use of natural and traditional therapies.

Dr. Parks has an MD from the University of Maryland and a master's degree in Public Health and Health Service Research from the University of California at Los Angeles (UCLA). He has completed specialty training in Internal Medicine at George Washington University, Preventive Medicine at UCLA, and Psychiatry at the University of Maryland. Dr. Parks is a former Assistant Professor at The Albany and University of Miami Medical School; Chief of Internal Medicine at the Homestead Air Force Base Hospital in Florida; former Director of the Center for Preventive and Nutritional Health Care in Baltimore, MD; and founder of Macro Health Medicine, a comprehensive and holistic consultative and treatment service formerly in Asheville, NC.

Through integrative psychiatry and medicine, he has treated addictions, ADHD, anxiety, bipolar illness, depression, panic disorder, post-trauma related illness (PTSD), eating disorders, family and relationship dysfunction, and spiritual emergence. An avid swimmer and an example of active, healthy living, Dr. Parks continues to advocate for an integrative approach to preventing, diagnosing, and treating physical and emotional problems.

A LETTER TO READERS

Dear Reader,

This note of appreciation goes to you who have read ***COVID-19/Mental Health Crises—Holistic Understanding & Solutions***. I hope there has been beneficial information for you or other people in your life .

If this book has been a beginning or support for you in your discovery, understanding, self-help, or healing, please continue your journey. Check out the book's resources or those from other trusted healthcare sources of information.

If you are in any distress related to the COVID pandemic or other significant challenges in your life, do seek out help and guidance. I have provided articles, information, some further resources, and a newsletter through my website and blog: **parksmd.com**

If you feel this book might benefit others, please leave a review on the site or outlet where you purchased the book.

For questions or if you like to send a review of the book that I can post on my website, please email me at **info@parksmd.com**

Thank you and sending you all my support for your journey of self-discovery and healing.

Ron Parks, MD

ENDNOTES

1   *The New York Times* (updated August 26, 2020). The U.S. surpasses 5 million cases. nytimes.com/2020/08/08/world/coronavirus-updates.html

Halverson, J.L., MD (Bienenfeld, D., MD, Chief Editor) (updated August 6, 2020). Depression, *Medscape.* emedicine.medscape.com/article/286759-overview

2   American Psychological Association, "Trauma", 2020, apa.org/topics/trauma

3   Centers for Disease Control and Prevention (September 1, 2020). *Helping children cope with emergencies.* cdc.gov/childrenindisasters/helping-children-cope.html

4   Sharp, J., MD (March 12, 2020). Coping with corona virus anxiety, *Harvard Health Publishing Blog.* apa.org/topics/trauma

Fader, S. (December 21, 2020). Trauma therapy: What is trauma therapy and how does it work to combat trauma? *Better Help.* betterhelp.com/advice/trauma/what-is-trauma-therapy-and-how-does-it-work

Centers for Disease Control and Prevention (March 19, 2018). *Coping with disaster or a traumatic event.* emergency.cdc.gov/coping/index.asp

5   Yasgur, B.S., LSW (August 12, 2020). Supplement plus probiotic may improve depressive symptoms, *Medscape Medical News.* medscape.com/viewarticle/935603

Brooks, M. (August 3, 2020). Depression, anxiety in COVID-19 indicators of CNS attack?, *Medscape Medical News.* medscape.com/viewarticle/935019

Centers for Disease Control and Prevention (December 11, 2020). *Coping with stress: Pandemics can be stressful.* cdc.gov/coronavirus/2019-ncov/daily-life-coping/managing-stress-anxiety.html

Centers for Disease Control and Prevention (September 12, 2019). *Taking care of your emotional health.* emergency.cdc.gov/coping/selfcare.asp

Centers for Disease Control and Prevention (March 19, 2018). *Emergency responders: Tips for taking care of yourself.* emergency.cdc.gov/coping/responders.asp

6   Benabio, J., MD (April 22, 2020). Overcoming COVID-related stress, *Medscape Psychiatry.* medscape.com/viewarticle/929166

Brooks, M. (March 26, 2020), COVID-19: 'striking' rates of anxiety, depression in healthcare workers, *Medscape Psychiatry*, medscape.com/viewarticle/927581

Brooks, M. (September 21, 2020). Surge in opioid overdoses linked to COVID-19, *Medscape Psychiatry.* medscape.com/viewarticle/937770

Browser, D. (September 25, 2020). Suicide, depression, anxiety: COVID 19's heavy toll on youth, *Medscape Psychiatry.* medscape.com/viewarticle/938065

National Institute of Mental Health (n.d.) *COVID-19 is an emerging, rapidly evolving situation.* nimh.nih.gov/health/education-awareness/shareable-resources-on-coping-with-covid-19.shtml

7   Kubler-Ross, Elizabeth. *On Death And Dying.* 1st ed. New York, NY: Scribner, 2014.

8   Legg, T.J., PhD, CRNP (June 3, 2020). Depression: facts, statistics, and you, *Healthline.* healthline.com/health/depression/facts-statistics-infographic

Depression and Bipolar Support Alliance (2020). *Depression statistics.* dbsalliance.org/education/depression/statistics

9   Ostaseski, Frank. *The Five Invitations: Discovering What Death Can Teach Us About Living Fully.* Reprint edition. New York, NY: Flatiron Books, 2019.

Nisargadatta, Maharaj. *I Am That.* 2nd American edition. Durham, NC; The Acorn Press (revised), 2012.

Rinpoche, Sogyal. *The Tibetan Book of Living and Dying: 25th Anniversary Edition* Paperback. USA: HarperSanFrancisco, 2020.

Hawkins, David R. *Letting Go: The Pathway of Surrender.* Vol. 9. 9 vols. *Power vs. Force.* USA: Veritas, 2013.

10   World Health Organization (December 8, 2020).
Coronavirus disease (COVID-19) advice for the public.
who.int/emergencies/diseases/novel-coronavirus-2019/advice-for-public

Centers for Disease Controls and Prevention (December 9, 2020). *Prevent getting sick.*
cdc.gov/coronavirus/2019-ncov/prevent-getting-sick/prevention.html

11   Asbill, B., MD (September 4, 2019). Ask the doctor: What Is lifestyle medicine?, *Mission Health blog,* Mission Health. blog.mission-health.org/2019/09/04/ask-the-doctor-what-is-lifestyle-medicine-brian-asbill-md-answers

12   Gaby, MD, Alan. *Nutritional Medicine.* 2nd Edition., 2017.

13   WorldHealth.Net (November 27, 2020). *Some of the benefits of exercise for those over 50,* worldhealth.net/news/some-benefits-exercise-those-over-50

14   Hedberg, N., DC. (2019). *A phased approach to COVID-19: Prevent to recovery,* Ashville: Immune Restoration Center. drhedberg.com/covid-19-prevention-recovery

Templeton, J. (2020). The 8 pillars of holistic health and wellness, *Ask the Scientists.* askthescientists.com/pillars-of-wellness

15   Lawlis, Frank, and Laura Martinez. *Psychoneuroplasticity Protocols for Addictions: A Clinical Companion for The Big Book.* Lanham, Md.: Rowman & Littlefield Publishers, 2015.

16   Center for Spiritual Emergence (n.d.), *Spiritual emergence/emergency,* 02/2021 centerforspiritualemergence.com/spiritual-emergenceemergency.html

17   Prendergast, John, and Dr. Peter Fenner. *Sacred Mirror: Nondual Wisdom and Psychotherapy.* St. Paul, Minnesota: Paragon House, 2003.

Prendergast, John, and Dr. Kenneth Bradford. *Listening from the Heart of Silence: Nondual Wisdom and Psychotherapy,.* Vol. 2 (Nondual Wisdom & Psychotherapy) Paperback. St. Paul, Minnesota: Pargon House, 2007.

Baugh, M. (2020). *The fourth wave of behaviorism: ACT, DBT, and non-dual wisdom,* New Perspectives Center for Counseling. sfnewperspectives.org/article-the-fourth-wave-of-behaviorism-act-dbt-and-nondual-wisdom

Fenner, P. (2017). radiantmind.net

18   Asbill, B, 2019.

19   Wikipedia (December 10, 2020). *Bipolar disorder,*
en.wikipedia.org/wiki/Bipolar_disorder

PsychGuides.com (2020). *Mental health disorder treatment guidelines and consumer guides,* psychguides.com

Depression and Bipolar Support Alliance (2020). dbsalliance.org

20   See also the references in the chapter "Bipolar Illness In Stressful Times." (pp. 78-82) of this book.

National Institute of Mental Health (NIMH) (January 2020). *Transforming the understanding and treatment of mental illnesses: information on bipolar disorder,* nimh.nih.gov/health/topics/bipolar-disorder/index.shtml

Vinitsky, A.R., and Parks, R.R. (December 10, 2012). Chapter 32: Bipolar disorder (pp. 595-615), in book by Kohlstadt (Ed.), Ingrid. *Advancing Medicine with Food and Nutrients* 2nd Edition. 2nd ed. : CRC Press, 2012.

Perlmutter MD, David, and Kristin Loberg. *Grain Brain: The Surprising Truth about Wheat, Carbs, and Sugar—Your Brain's Silent Killers.* (Hardcover), Revised. New York, Boston, London: Little,Brown, Spark, 2018.

21   Brooks, M. (October 3, 2019). Antidepressants are safe: Final word?, *Medscape Psychiatry.* medscape.com/viewarticle/919413

Lesage, A., and Diallo, F.B. (2016). Prenatal antidepressant use and risk of autism spectrum disorders in children, *JAMA Pediatrics, 170*(2), 117-124. jamanetwork.com/journals/jamapediatrics/article-abstract/2476187

Lunghi, C., et al. (May 7, 2020). Prevalence and determinants of long-term utilization of antidepressant drugs: A retrospective cohort study, *Neuropsychiatric Disease and Treatment, 16*, 1157–1170. ncbi.nlm.nih.gov/pmc/articles/PMC7213896

Simon, G.E., MD, et al. (January 1, 2006). Suicide risk during antidepressant treatment, *American Journal of Psychiatry.* ajp.psychiatryonline.org/doi/full/10.1176/appi.ajp.163.1.41

Casper, R.C., MD; Fleisher, B.E., MD; Lee-Ancajas, J.C., Ph.D.; Gilles, A., et al. (April 2003). Follow-up of children of depressed mothers exposed or not exposed to antidepressant drugs during pregnancy, *The Journal of Pediatrics, 142*(4), 402-408. sciencedirect.com/science/article/abs/pii/S0022347603000404

Rai, D., Lee, B.K., Dalman, C., Golding, J., Glyn, L., and Magnusson, C. (April 19, 2013). Parental depression, maternal antidepressant use during pregnancy, and risk of autism spectrum disorders: population-based case-control study, *BMJ, 2013;346:f2059.* bmj.com/content/346/bmj.f2059.short

Sørensen, M.J., Grønborg, T.K., Christensen, J., Parner, T.T., et al. (November 15, 2013). Antidepressant exposure in pregnancy and risk of autism spectrum disorders, *Clinical Epidemiology, 5,* 449–459. ncbi.nlm.nih.gov/pmc/articles/PMC383238

22   American Psychiatric Association. *Desk Reference to the Diagnostic Criteria from DSM-5.* Arlington, VA.: American Psychiatric Publishing, 2013.

23   The National Institute of Mental Health (n.d.), *Mental health information.* nimh.nih.gov/health/index.shtml

National Institute of Mental Health (n.d.). *Bipolar disorder.* nimh.nih.gov/health/topics/bipolar-disorder/index.shtml

Anxiety and Depression Association of America (2020). *Coronavirus anxiety: Helpful expert tips and resources,* adaa.org

Vinitsky and Parks (2012).

24   American Psychiatric Association. Desk Reference to the Diagnostic Criteria from DSM-5. Arlington, VA.: American Psychiatric Publishing, 2013.

25   Dr. Lindenfield (January 3, 2017). *RESET Therapy.* drlindenfeldresettherapy.com/ptsd

26   U.S. Department of Veterans Affairs National Center for PTSD (October 17, 2019). How common is PTSD in adults?, ptsd.va.gov/understand/common/common_adults.asp

U.S. Department of Veterans Affairs National Center for PTSD (February 15, 2019). *Understand PTSD,* ptsd.va.gov/understand/index.asp

Ghaemi, N., MD, MPH (November 6, 2015). Trauma that isn't trauma: PTSD and the science of causation, *Medscape Psychiatry.* medscape.com/viewarticle/853536?nlid=91226_4210

Social Security Administration (n.d.). *PTSD fact sheet,* ssa.gov/disability/Documents/PTSD%20Fact%20Sheet.pdf

27   National Center for Drug Abuse Statistics (2019). *Drug abuse statistics,* drugabusestatistics.org

28   National Institute on Drug Abuse (May 27, 2020). *Opioid overdose crisis,* drugabuse.gov/drug-topics/opioids/opioid-overdose-crisis

North Carolina Department of Health and Human Services (July 2020). *Opioid-involved overdoses, 2018,* injuryfreenc.ncdhhs.gov/DataSurveillance/poisoning/OpioidFactsheet-2018-FINAL.pdf

29 American Society of Addiction Medicine (ASAM) (2020). Definition of addiction, asam.org/quality-practice/definition-of-addiction

30 Psychiatry Online (2020). *DSM library*, dsm.psychiatryonline.org

31 Substance Abuse and Mental Health Services Administration (April 30, 2020). *Mental health and substance use disorders*, samhsa.gov/find-help/disorders

TTTrx Opioid Recovery Resources (n.d.). turnthetiderx.org

National Institute on Drug Abuse (n.d.). *Alcohol Use Disorders Identification Test (AUDIT)*, drugabuse.gov/sites/default/files/audit.pdf

32 Lawlis and Martinez, 2015.

33 Center for Spiritual Emergence, 2017.

34 Parks, R., MD (2020). *Addiction resources*, parksmd.com/addiction-references-resources

Substance Abuse Mental Health Service Administration (SAMHSA), 2020.

Mercola, J., M.D. (April 15, 2017). *Chasing the dragon—America's struggle with opioid addiction*, articles.mercola.com/sites/articles/archive/2017/04/15/documentary-chasing-the-dragon-opioid-addiction.aspx

35 McCance-Katz, E.F., MD, PhD (2018). *The national survey on drug use and health: 2017*, Substance Abuse and Mental Health Services Administration. samhsa.gov/data/sites/default/files/nsduh-ppt-09-2018.pdf

36 O'Brien, B. (July 23, 2018). What is citta in Buddhism?, *Learn religions*. learnreligions.com/citta-449530

37 Kornfield, Jack. *No Time Like the Present: Finding Freedom, Love, and Joy Right Where You Are*. New York, NY: Atria Books, 2017.

Beck, J. (August 4, 2016). In a brain age, the heart retains its symbolic power, *The Atlantic*. theatlantic.com/health/archive/2016/08/the-enduring-metaphors-of-the-heart-this-mortal-coil-fay-bound-alberti/494375

38 Kübler-Ross, 2014.

39 American Sleep Association (2020). *Stages of sleep: The sleep cycle*, sleepassociation.org/about-sleep/stages-of-sleep

40 Spira, Rupert. *The Nature of Consciousness: Essays on the Unity of Mind and Matter*. Paperback. 1st ed. Oxford: Sahja Publications Oxford, n.d.

41   Sri Nisargadatta Maharaj, 2012.

42   Hawkins, David R. Power vs. Force: The Hidden Determinants of Human Behavior. Kindle. Vol. 1. 8 vols. Power vs. Force. Veritas; 1st edition, 2013.

43   Klein, Jean, and Emma Edwards. *The Ease of Being.* Paperback. United Kingdom: New Sarum Press, 2020.

44   Campbell, Joseph. *The Power of Myth.* Paperback. New York, NY: Anchor., 1991.

Jung, C.G. Memories, *Dreams, Reflections.* Paperback, Revised ed. New York: Vintage Books, 1989.

45   Center for Spiritual Emergence (n.d.). centerforspiritualemergence.com

46   Miller, M., MD (February 13, 2015).
The relevance of twelve-step recovery in 21st century addiction medicine, *Quality & Science.* asam.org/Quality-Science/publications/magazine/read/article/2015/02/13/the-relevance-of-twelve-step-recovery-in-21st-century-addiction-medicine

47   Organizations providing relief assistance:

Feeding America: feedingamerica.org

UNICEF USA: unicefusa.org/donate

World Vision, Inc.: worldvision.org

American Red Cross : redcross.org/donate/donation.html

48   Della Cava, M. (March 21, 2020). For those who survived polio, coronavirus is eerily familiar. But ultimately, 'science won', *USA Today.* usatoday.com/story/news/nation/2020/03/21/coronavirus-quarantine-haunts-polio-epidemic-survivors/2868771001

Wikipedia (December 19, 2020). *Elizabeth Kenny.* en.wikipedia.org/wiki/Elizabeth_Kenny

Wikipedia (December 9, 2020). *Polio.* en.wikipedia.org/wiki/Polio

Wikipedia (December 3, 2020). History of polio. en.wikipedia.org/wiki/History_of_polio

Sokol, B. (1997). Fear of polio in the 1950s, *The beat begins: America in the 1950s.* plosin.com/beatbegins/projects/sokol.html

49   Tumin, R., and Walker, E. (June 28, 2020). The number of new coronavirus cases in the U.S. and COVID-19 can spread without symptoms, *The New York Times: The Morning.*

Whyte, J. MD, MPH; Lieberman, J.A., MD; Mayer; and L.S., MD (May 15, 2020). *The mental health aftermath of COVID-19*, Medscape Psychiatry. medscape.com/viewarticle/930528

Sanger-Katz, M.; Miller, Claire C.; Bui, Q. (June 8, 2020). When 511 epidemiologists expect to fly, hug and do 18 other everyday activities again, *The New York Times: The Upshot.* nytimes.com/interactive/2020/06/08/upshot/when-epidemiologists-will-do-everyday-things-coronavirus.html

50   Parker-Pope, T. (June 9, 2020). Five rules to live by during a pandemic, *The New York Times.* nytimes.com/2020/06/09/well/live/coronavirus-rules-pandemic-infection-prevention. html

Manson, J.E., MD, DrPH (May 11, 2020). Does Vitamin D protect against COVID-19?, *Medscape Psychiatry.* medscape.com/viewarticle/930152

WorldHealth.net (June 8, 2020). *Typical Western diet found to impair brain function & appetite control,* worldhealth.net/news/typical-western-diet-found-impair-brain-function-appetite-control

51   Parks, R., MD (2020). *About integrative & holistic approaches,* parksmd.com/about-2/about-integrative-and-holistic-approaches

52   Skodol, A., MD (2020). Overview of personality disorders, *Merck manual professional version*, Merck, Sharp & Dohme Corp. merckmanuals.com/professional/psychiatric-disorders/personality-disorders/overview-of-personality-disorders

American Psychiatric Association, 2013.

53   Lighter, J., et al. (August 1, 2020). Obesity in patients younger than 60 years is a risk factor for COVID-19 hospital admission, *Clinical Infectious Diseases*, 71(15), 896–897. academic.oup.com/cid/article/71/15/896/5818333

Holmes, R. (March 25, 2020). COVID-19 likely worse for vapers, smokers, *HealthDay News*, WebMD. webmd.com/lung/news/20200325/covid-19-likely-worse-for-vapers-smokers

54   Gore, Al., *An Inconvenient Truth: The Crisis of Global Warming.* Paperback, Revised Ed. New York, NY: Viking Books for Young Readers., 2007.

55   Wadman, M., et al. (April 17, 2020). How does Coronavirus kill? Clinicians trace a ferocious rampage through the body, from the brain to toes, *Science*. sciencemag.org/news/2020/04/how-does-coronavirus-kill-clinicians-trace-ferocious-rampage-through-body-brain-toes

Hedberg, N., 2019.

Rossoff, M., L.Ac. (2020). *Preparing for the coronavirus, also known as COVID-19.* michaelrossoff.com/preparing-for-the-coronavirus.html

Thich Nhat, Hanh. *Peace Is Every Step: The Path of Mindfulness in Everyday Life.* English, Paperback. New York, NY.: Bantam Books, 1992.

56   Manson, J.E., 2020.

WorldHealth.net, June 8, 2020.

57   Whyte, J. MD, et al. (May 15, 2020).

58   Thich Nhat, Hanh. (March 1, 1992).

Fountain, H. (May 18, 2020).
Climate change is making hurricanes stronger, researchers find, *The New York Times*. nytimes.com/2020/05/18/climate/climate-changes-hurricane-intensity.html

Sanger-Katz, M., et al. (June 8, 2020).

59   Conze, Edward. *Buddhism: Its Essence and Development.* Paperback, English. New York, NY: Dover Publications, Inc., 2003.

Wilber, Ken. *The Essential Ken Wilber: An Introductory Reader.* Paperback, English. Boston, London: Shambhala, 1998.

Grof, S., and C. Grof. *Holotropic Breath Work: A New Approach to Self-Exploration and Therapy.* Excelsior First Printing. Albany: State of New York University Press, 2010.

Iyengar, B.K.S. Iyengar, B.K.S. *Light On Yoga: The Classic Guide to Yoga by the World's Foremost Authority.* Paperback, English. Harper Collins, 2006.

Carse, David. *Perfect Brilliant Stillness: Beyond the Individual Self.* Paperback, English. Paragate Publishing, 2006.

Klein, J. *I Am.* English, 1st edition. United Kingdom: Non-Duality Press, 2006.

Watts, Alan. Psychotherapy East & West. Paperback, English. Novato, CA.: New World Library, 2017.

Sivananda Yoga Center, and Devananda, V. *The Sivananda Companion to Yoga: A Complete Guide to the Physical Postures, Breathing Exercises, Diet, Relaxation, and Meditation of Yoga.* 1st Fireside Edition. Atria Books, 2000.

Ostaseski, January 22, 2019.

Wilber, Ken. *Integral Meditation: Mindfulness as a Way to Grow up, Wake up, and Show up in Your Life.* Illustrated edition. Boulder: Shambhala, 2016.

Isherwood, C. *Vedanta for the Western World.* Paperback, English. Andesite Press, 2017.

60   Parks, R., MD. (2020). *Remembering the holocaust.* parksmd.com/remembering-the-holocaust

Made in the USA
Coppell, TX
19 October 2022